ALGORITHMS,
BLOCKCHAIN &
CRYPTOCURRENCY

THE FUTURE OF WORK

The future of work is a vital contemporary area of debate both in business and management research, but also in wider social, political and economic discourse. Global relevant issues, including the ageing workforce, rise of the gig economy, workplace automation and changing forms of business ownership are all regularly the subject of discussion in both academic research and the mainstream media, with wider professional and public policy implications.

The Future of Work series features books examining key issues or challenges in the modern workplace, synthesising prior developments in critical thinking, alongside current practical challenges in order to interrogate possible future developments in the world of work.

Offering future research agendas and suggesting practical outcomes for today's and tomorrow's businesses and workforce, the books in this series present powerful, challenging and polemical analysis of a diverse range of subjects in their potential to address future challenges and possible new trajectories.

The series highlights what changes still need to be made to core areas of business practice and theory in order for them to be forward facing, more representative, and able to fulfil the industrial challenges of the future.

Other Titles in the Series

Careers: Thinking, Strategising and Prototyping
Ann M. Brewer

Forthcoming Titles

Workforce Health and Productivity
Stephen Bevan and Cary L. Cooper

Spending Without Thinking: The Future of Consumption
Richard Whittle

Personnel Selection: Finding the Future of Talent Through Science and Technology
Tomas Chamorro-Premuzic, Franziska Leutner and Reece Akhtar

Cooperatives at Work
George Cheney, Matt Noyes and Emi Do

ALGORITHMS, BLOCKCHAIN & CRYPTOCURRENCY

Implications for the Future of the Workplace

GAVIN BROWN
Manchester Metropolitan University, UK

and

RICHARD WHITTLE
Manchester Metropolitan University, UK

United Kingdom – North America – Japan – India
Malaysia – China

Emerald Publishing Limited
Howard House, Wagon Lane, Bingley BD16 1WA, UK

First edition 2020

British Library Cataloguing in Publication Data
A catalogue record for this book is available from the British
Library

ISBN: 978-1-83867-498-4 (Print)
ISBN: 978-1-83867-495-3 (Online)
ISBN: 978-1-83867-497-7 (Epub)

ISOQAR certified
Management System,
awarded to Emerald
for adherence to
Environmental
standard
ISO 14001:2004.

Certificate Number 1985
ISO 14001

INVESTOR IN PEOPLE

CONTENTS

LIST OF TABLES AND FIGURES

INTRODUCTION

Welcome to this book In *Algorithms, Blockchain & Cryptocurrency: Implications for the Future of the Workplace*, we are taking a long position on the eventual future effects of the combination of three (and the many more accompanying) technologies, which in our view will combine to produce a world of work entirely alien to what we currently recognise. In this world, we imagine considerable, if not total, platform-based self-employment facilitated by blockchain-based smart contracts and remunerated by global cryptocurrencies. We would hope that this does not become a simple race to the bottom, as history would prophesise, but in fact through a partnership with the state and unions, becomes a future where workers' rights and conditions are improved and inequality decreases. A big ask considering historical precedent, but one that we believe is possible. However, ultimately excess profitability which arises from a new style of working, must be (mostly) reallocated to the worker, and this is where the state must come in.

In this book, we will provide a very general introduction to the key concepts including a working knowledge and understanding of the algorithmising process, the blockchain and cryptocurrencies. It must be remembered that the march of technological process continues to far outstrip our ability to pin down long-term definitions, so as a note of warning to the reader, please remember that as the concepts of algorith-mising, blockchain and in particular cryptocurrency evolve in their application to the world of work, so our understanding of their effects is must. Indeed in the writing of this book, the understanding of the effect of cryptocurrency on the world of work and the worker has far outpaced the ability of regula-tors and interest groups to keep up.

When we first considered this book and developing our understanding of the effect of cryptocurrency, we were in effect dealing with what we know understand as first and second generation cryptocurrency. Cryptos which in effect attempted to become monies in their own right, but were fun-damentally unable to fulfil the required monetary functions due to their price volatility, and then cryptocurrency which tokenised and quantified activity and behaviours, but which were not necessarily intended for use outside of bespoke and niche (though often grand in scope and imagination) areas. As the book progressed so did cryptocurrencies, the notion of a corporate cryptocurrency incorporating a stable price design came to the fore, this in particular begins to shake the very foundations of our current world of work, and much of the future of work in this book is facilitated by the idea of a stable global cryptocurrency. However, all things continue to change, and the latest developments at the time of writ-ing suggest that this idea has stalled under intense regulatory scrutiny, with the future of money in this space, being a devo-lution in price stability but an increase in decentralisation with a move back towards first-generation cryptocurrency, or an increase in price stability with a decrease in decentralisa-tion with a movement towards central bank digital currency. Ultimately though, we consider that whatever form the future of cryptocurrency takes, an eventual outcome will be a price stable widely accepted coins, and those coins will have a strik-ing effect on the world of work.

In order to help understand this new world from the perspective of the worker, we overweight our analysis based on cryptocurrency, we consider that whilst they may eventually have a greater if not more subtle effect, the 'back-office' functions of algorithms and blockchain, whilst they provide the structure and facilitation of a new world of work, they do not provide its face. The worker in this new world of work will interact with the platform and receive remuneration in a new currency (or currencies). In this future, the worker may well feel far more connected to their online world than the state. In this future, algorithms decide what work is needed, blockchain provides the security to the organisation and the worker and crypto facilitates payment.

Again, we must note the evolution of technology during the progress of this work, algorithmising continues to outpace expectation, and predictions from our childhoods around robotic doctors, automated assistants and artificial decision making, may be merely a few years away. The assistant on your smartphone or in your email which is helping you with dinner plans, travel arrangements or even to decide your next purchase was unimaginable even a few years ago. If you can think back to voice dialling on the first phone you had, and consider now, where you could be interacting with a bot online, conversing with your phone or household smart speaker or listening to artificial intelligence (AI) composed music. The progression is amazing and it is only getting faster. Likewise, the key concept of blockchain for this book, that of an unimaginable number of continually actioned, instantaneously generated, legally watertight contracts, is only just being explored and we would guess that there are far more applications to come. Of course, this may as yet come to naught, the blockchain world is still in its infancy and a small number of high-profile security breaches, privacy issues or misuses could, like corporate cryptocurrencies, derail its trajectory. However, we note that part of the secret of innovation is simply knowing what once was impossible is now possible and like cryptocurrency, the end effect is in sight, even if the route to it is more murky. This end of a global, instant and cheap, microcontract world can now exist to facilitate a world of work very different to what we are presently used to.

The effect of technology on all our working lives continues to be underestimated, indeed the reader of this book may well be based at a research institution, think tank or be a working professional with a sought after skill set, which one may think immune to the ongoing march of automation. However, please consider this. One of the above paragraphs was mostly written by algorithm, using a simple email autocomplete function, again the function which makes our lives more convenient, helping us answer texts and emails, guessing our online searches or products we'd like to buy, makes a very good attempt at completing a block of prose. Of course, this was not perfect and required human oversight and editing, but the action of writing, of transferring our human thoughts to word was sped up, refined and supported by technology. In terms of an academic article, realistically how far away are we from an automated research assistant which will (at least) complete the literature review and data analysis. At least for a while, the human element is needed to direct and conceptualise the research, however a future where every possible combination of variable and test is run on a dataset, the most effective tests and significant relationships are selected and an automated academic article framework is produced to accompany them. Even a simple clumsy autocomplete algorithm can in time and with training develop into a substitute for highly skilled and complex labour.

Again history let's see how even established organisations and professions can fall to the march of technological progress. Probably, the most relevant examples are the Industrial

Revolution and the development of the internet, both of which we discuss at length in this book. The Industrial Revolution wholly transformed our ideas of work, even of time and society, the development of the internet exacerbated those changes. In this book, we propose changes similar in scope to these events, our future of work is one where ideas of time, output, money and even a job are again wholly redefined. Of particular relevance here is the parallel with finance, we explore a framework of technological progression in financial services in order to further understand the effect of these technologies on the world of work. We propose that the technological evolution of finance, that of Traditional Financial Institutions → FinTech → TechFin, can provide considerable insight for the developments in and destination of the world of work, and is a good way to conceptualise the current seismic changes in the world of work.

If we imagine that traditional financial services represent the usual post-Industrial Revolution view of work, then Fin-Tech represents the technological development of work within the traditional infrastructure and TechFin represents the evolution of this development outside the traditional infrastructure. The phenomenon is still the same, be it financial services or work, but crucially the structure and organisation which delivers this output is practically unrecognisable to what has gone before. If we take the analogy of a mortgage, in traditional finance you went to the bank to request it and after a labour intensive and generally inefficient evaluation process, you got a decision. In the FinTech era, you still went to the bank, but perhaps online or via a phone appointment, and various back-office systems sped up the process, to the extent where in the previous traditional route, the decision which may have taken a month, now takes a few days. In the TechFin era, you may ask a big tech firm for a mortgage, which will provide you with an instant decision based on your online activity. Likewise, in our world of work, in a traditional sense, you worked in an organisation or institution, in the FinTech sense you worked in the same infrastructure with productivity increased with technology, and in the Tech-Fin sense you work in a wholly different infrastructure. You may log into your platform and conduct remote process jobs, your work may be a series of interviews to help marketing algorithms learn the essence of a product or online interactions to evaluate AI creative content. The output of work is the same, the route to it is wholly different.

If the route to work is wholly different, then we must alter our definition of worker. If we currently view the idea of a worker as an individual who within our infrastructure trades time for money, then in many ways we perhaps need to revert to a pre-Industrial Revolution idea of work, which is output based and not time dependent. The weaver who in a particular batch of wool found it easy to work with and their output took half the time as normal, received the same remuneration as a week where the batch was difficult to work and the output took and extra day. Platform working is in some ways more similar to that, where a freelance web designer charges the same for a project it takes them half the time to complete compared to their slower rival for the work. This is closer to a pre-industrial work pattern than a post-industrial one, where a factory worker (at least for a time) received the same weekly wage, regardless of output.

A new way of working, naturally brings into consideration what necessary changes are required to our training and skill development, including discussions around how best to school a population for ideas of highly global mobile working. Indeed, consideration here must be made of avoiding a race to the bottom where skill development and surplus result in a diminishing wage and condition and specialised bespoke training, be it through private provision or elite institutions is the only route to success. Throughout this book, we consider that the benefits of this new world of work should be accessible, available and distributed to all, and again here we see the state as necessary in this. Frequently with the discussion of the globalised market place, online work and decentralisation of currency and information, the role of the state appears expected to diminish. In our view, the state must provide a bulwark protecting the worker and reenergise and reinvigorate itself from its gradual decline. Whereas the 'FinTech like' evolution of work potentially pushed the state out of this sphere, the 'TechFin like' evolution of work must bring a stronger role for the state and unions to protect the worker. We would hope that, against the current precarious nature of platform working, mass work in this fashion would provide considerable opportunity for mass platform unionisation, facilitated by blockchain organisation.

1

NOW I KNOW MY ABC (ALGORITHMS, BLOCKCHAIN AND CRYPTOCURRENCY)

INTRODUCTION

This chapter presents an introduction to algorithms, blockchain and cryptocurrency (ABC) and discusses their implications for the world of work. In particular, we note that it is the convergence of these new technologies that have the paradigm-shifting effect.

ALGORITHMS AND WORK

We begin this book with a gentle explainer to the main technologies. In the following sections, the introductions to ABC and their respective implications for work are intended to be, as non-technical as possible, introductions to the individual technologies. Several excellent, more technical, explanations exist in the literature, but for the purposes of this book, we want anyone regardless of their technical familiarity to be gently introduced to ABC and their respective implications for the world of work.

An Introduction to Algorithms

Algorithms seem to be an opaque and impenetrable concept; however, fundamentally they are simply a precise set of instructions to complete a task or process, generate an output, or simply turn A into B. Algorithms are everywhere, making the technology we use work and governing our simple decisions. Whilst the ones running your phone, payments, computer, car and so on are often unimaginably complex, the concept itself is delightfully simple. Simply, an algorithm is a precise set of instructions or formula for solving a problem or doing a task. In a computing sense, we use algorithms to tell a computer how to do a given task.

When we consider any algorithm as a set of precise instructions and not simply as a purely computational topic, we can see that algorithms are simply all around us. Recipes are algorithms, transactions are algorithms, as is the process of cleaning your home, solving an equation or even your daily commute.

As described above, a useful way to grasp the idea of framing an algorithm is to write your own commute as an algorithm. Soon you will be using important computational concepts such as repetition (brake when red light, gas when green), sequencing (board bus then pay) and conditional logic (if sunny, walk). With practice and precision, you will be able to accurately create an algorithm for your commute that others could follow. Part of the skill, though, is getting a computer to follow these instructions; another human following your commute instructions will have an inherent knowledge which can cover the imprecision in your instructions. For example, board bus and pay; is a human instruction which covers all aspects of interaction and a multitude of different scenarios. However, it doesn't specify, for example, a request for 'exact change only', an unspecified queueing scenario, and so on. A human would know what to do in these situations; unless it is specified in the algorithm, a computer would not have an appropriate response.

However, we can see with increasing complexity that any process or task can be broken down into a series of instructions or commands. In this book, we assume that most if not all work will be algorithmised, and we term each instruction a microtask.

Algorithms and Work

With advances in artificial intelligence (AI), robotics, augmented reality, sensors and the increasing real-world presence of technology, computers are simply able to do tasks that are previously considered only achievable by a human more efficiently, cheaper and more consistently. We no longer even need to produce the initial programming, machines can learn to do this themselves.

Crucially, now every time a human completes a task, there is a massive data generation which allows computers to learn how to do it better. In this book, we suggest that the algorithmising of tasks will create a series of microtasks – most of the tasks to be done by machine and some to be done by human workers – creating additional microtasks for humans. Ultimately, we suggest that the work which will be displaced by machines will be replaced and also suggest that the work which will be displaced by machines will be replaced with a form of work we term Bitworking – the completions of microtasks as a work activity rather than the skilled completion of a singular process. In an algorithmised machine learning world, each microtask has a shelf life as the data generated by its completion are analysed and the optimum way found, generating other microtasks and so on.

Key Points:

1. Most if not all tasks can be conceptualised as algorithms.

2. Advances in AI mean that this process accelerates until we get to the fundamental set of microtasks for any specific output.

3. Machines can do most but not all microtasks.

4. Work will be displaced by algorithms but not destroyed, complementary work will be developed as well as microtasks designed specifically by machines for humans.

BLOCKCHAIN AND WORK

What Is Blockchain?

Wikipedia tells us that

> *A blockchain, originally blockchain, is a growing list of records, called blocks, that are linked using cryptography. Each block contains a cryptographic hash of the previous block, a timestamp, and transaction data.*

What does this mean?

In order to understand this, we need to actually go back in time quite far. The first example of double-entry bookkeeping found in 1494 by a Franciscan Friar, Luca Pacioli. This was hugely important as it generated sound recording of credits and debits. Jumping forwards, in 2018, the paper on Bitcoin (Nakamoto, 2008) was equally ground breaking as it created an electronic currency, aka cryptocurrency, namely Bitcoin, and with it solving the double-spending problem which had so far plagued online money operating without the need for regulated trust authority. The Bitcoin White Paper suggested a ledger distributed via peer-to-peer networks recording trans-actions in blocks, each block giving validation by different node computers in the network, and this validation is gen-erated by solving cryptographic mathematical problems also called hashes. Following this, each next block is stamped with a new cryptographic hash and is visible to all. Whatever data recorded in the new block are immutable and cannot really be altered unless all preceding blocks are changed by the agree-ment of the network majority. This is called blockchain, and it is the foundational technology of Bitcoin and cryptocurrency. However, blockchain is more than just cryptocurrency, it is a brand new technology which has the potential to revolution-ise all storage transmission of data. Later in this book, we will look at how, in effect, everything can be broken down to data, and we will look at the long-term trend of digitisation of our lives, but for now let's just remember that blockchain has the potential to ultimately transform everything that can be bro-ken down to 1s and 0s. Blockchain technology can provide more efficient storage, more efficient stock markets, border transactions, government records and so on. Blockchain tech-nology can change the entire way we operate, through the creation of decentralised autonomous organisations (DAOs) which perform automatic actions in specific circumstances by using smart contracts. The previous unexciting jargon heavy sentence quite simply means that through an exten-sion of blockchain technology we can eradicate the need for stocks and shares, insurance products, potentially banking as a whole and several aspects of government governance and regulation. Blockchain is certainly being regarded as a game changer with a significant number of ground-breaking applications and as a complement to the AI, algorithms and new technology impacts the future of work enormously.

Let's try to pinpoint in the idea of what blockchain actually is. We first became aware of it as the underlying technology of Bitcoin. Blockchain is a combination of two existing processes, namely distributed ledger technology and cryptography. In order to understand this, we will look at how Bitcoin works. Bitcoin does not store the information, the data and the processes in any one place, but it stores the same in numerous identical places. If we consider what we think of as a ledger, we generally think of a place like a bank or an insurance firm. A bank where is money stored is one place with just a single ledger. On the other side of the spectrum, what we know of as distributed ledgers, the information, the data and the processes are stored over several locations. Blockchain is a distributed ledger technology which is cryptographically protected. Cryptography is the process of secure moving and storage of data by encryption. People may be familiar with the developments of cryptography particularly in the context of the Second World War and the events at Bletchley Park. Blockchain is a combination of distributed ledger technology and cryptography, that is, a system of highly secure distributed ledgers.

Indeed, all this cryptography and multiple blocks make it very hard to break those blocks, thus making it a very secure system (but of course anything that is secure now may not be very soon!). The way blockchain is constructed means everything is recorded permanently, meaning that there is always a full and traceable history. Therefore, going back to Bitcoin lodged on the blockchain, we can take any single Bitcoin and view its entire life story, and we can look at it from when it was mined and every movement it has ever made, every account it has ever been transferred into. Blockchain is also transparent in an open blockchain such that anyone can see what is going on. Blockchain has the potential to fundamentally affect the world of work. Whilst it is required to support the cryptocurrency aspects that we consider in this book, it has an additionally and potentially even more ground-breaking property. Earlier we mentioned smart contracts; these are the real gamechangers produced by blockchain and their effects are still being explored and are yet to be fully understood.

A smart contract is an automated contract which uses predefined rules to govern the exchange of virtually any good or service. The key aim is to produce a transparent, unambiguous and low fee transaction. The smart contract is unambiguous as all terms are predefined and it enforces itself by following a predetermined and predefined process. Smart contracts are exceptionally low cost and give cast-iron certainty to each party. In this book, we consider that smart contracts are a key disrupter of the world of work as they hugely enable increased worker and organisation flexibility, whilst maintaining (and even increasing) trust between them.

What Can a Smart Contract Do?

To recap, a smart contract is an instruction based on blockchain specifically designed to improve the existing notion of a contract. A block contains this instruction, namely inputs and outputs, and heavily reduces the need for intermediation and so costs. There is no chance of misinterpretation as the contract is run on logic and predefined highly specific terms. Later in this book, we require the flexibility and trust of a smart contract to allow for increased worker mobility and flexibility whilst increasing the trust in contractual fulfilment.

If a worker completes a specific input for a firm anywhere in the world, with a smart contract, they know for certain what their reward will be, when and how it will arrive, as well as knowing all conditions of the contract in a wholly transparent and unambiguous way.

Blockchain and Work

We can see that virtually in every area where there is an exchange, there is potential for disruption by smart contracts run on blockchain. However, in our view, the widespread disruption to the world of work comes from smart contracts facilitating global flexible exchange of input and reward between any worker and any organisation. A worker, performing any short term, microtask for any organisation will have the security of an unambiguous contract. An organisation will be able to provide this security without the costs associated with intermediation. An organisation may generate countless million smart contracts a day to provide security for all volumes and amounts of payments. Let's consider a worker completing several hundred microtasks a day for very low-level payments. A smart contract would give each low-level payment the security of a full contract, currently unimaginable and uneconomic. This new ability to provide full trust and full security for any task, no matter how small or low value, provides the foundation for the idea of the new world of work presented in this book.

Though it must be remembered, we are looking at a future where blockchain fulfils its potential. Davidson, De Filippi, and Potts (2018, p. 641) consider that

> a case can be made that blockchains are indeed a general purpose technology that will improve the productive efficiency of some economic operations.

Furthermore respect of the hype (high), or levels of adoption (growing, but still very low), or the actual speed and cost of each transaction (for instance, with the current block size constraints and without the use of side chains, Bitcoin is still orders of magnitude slower and more costly than global payment platforms such as MasterCard\Visa or PayPal), blockchain is plainly a technology that will lower the transaction costs of some exchanges.

In short, blockchain has the potential, but the hype is currently far greater than the reality. Davidson et al. (2018, p. 641) go on to argue that

those who take a long position in blockchain are in effect arguing that it will improve the efficiency of economic systems by disintermediating many current patterns of exchange and production, thus improving economic efficiency.

This book takes a similar long position on blockchain, and central to our forecasts of the future of work is blockchain fulfilling its potential – that is, making good its current hype.

CRYPTOCURRENCY AND ITS IMPLICATIONS FOR WORK

What the Hell Are Cryptocurrencies?

In 2008, the pseudonymous Satoshi Nakamoto developed

an electronic payment system based on cryptographic proof instead of trust, allowing any two willing parties to transact directly with each other without the need for a trusted third party.

In short, they created a monetary system without the need for banks, regulation or government. This system is called Bitcoin – it is probably what you recognise when we talk about cryptocurrencies. However, several dozen (at least) cryptocurrencies or coins and tokens have come into existence and vanished since 2008. These coins and tokens are usually developed as an attempt to replicate the functions of money or provide a specific new service mechanism or function, for example, the transmission of data records or data. The key is getting a cryptocurrency accepted and this is assumed to be a function of the market, if you have people who trust the currency then it becomes accepted, if there is a good use case then it becomes accepted. The cryptocurrency must convince the public that it can do what it promised and that is has value. Spithoven (2019) states that cryptocurrency ecosystem include the initiators, codebase, programmers, miners, middlemen, customers, the media and government.

In order to get a feel for how cryptocurrencies work, we will look at three aspects of this cryptocurrency ecosystem, namely the code base, the programmers and the middlemen, and we will look at Bitcoin as a good example of how cryptocurrencies work. The code behind Bitcoin is common and the fact that it is open source enables everyone to make proposals to change it. The trust that is necessary in a sovereign currency world is produced via decentralised public ledges, known as the blockchain. We covered blockchain in the previous section in more detail, but for now we will use the Halpern (2018) definition, which is a system to share information and to store the history of transactions on a computer network.

Then, the code is open source and facilitated by the Blockchain, a community of programmers coordinate (regulate) the Bitcoin Protocol, and miners produce the Bitcoin. The key aspect from the customer facing view of cryptocurrency is the middlemen. Cryptocurrencies need a full suite of intermediaries between themselves and the customer in order to facilitate their operation. Customers in the UK don't usually deal on a one-to-one basis with the Bank of England or the Treasury, and in the cryptoworld, customers don't usually deal directly with the code, programmers or miners. They use intermediaries, and a cryptocurrency wallet can be thought of as a bank account for the purposes of this book.

For this book, then, we want you to think of cryptocurrencies as private forms of money which (will eventually) replicate the functions of money but have much more flexibility. They can be issued by anyone and only those who have value survive. The cryptographic proof aspect provides trust, but the currencies that survive will become as trusted as established sovereign currencies over time. Middlemen provide services similar to our existing financial infrastructure and in time flexible cryptocurrencies will be as accepted as sovereign currency.

The next development of cryptocurrencies is of equal importance to our analysis of their effect on the future of work. The corporate-crypto-coins are so-called 'cryptocorps'.

Corporate-crypto-coins

Currently, the United Nations recognises 180 currencies, each and every one of them is issued by a nation state. It does not recognise cryptocurrencies as legal tender. The idea of corporate-issued cryptocurrencies however are developing an interesting and challenging third area. Facebook's Libra is the first cryptocurrency with enough heft to punch into the global currency classification.

Facebook counts around half the global population as active monthly users: 2.2 billion on Facebook, 0.8 billion on Instagram and 0.7 billion on WhatsApp. This will instantly take holders and users of the currency into the biggest financial services firm in history, with more users than the US dollar. Coupled with the stable coin design of Libra, the first true global currency could be soon with us.

The standard and justified criticism of cryptocurrencies is that they don't fulfil the three essential characteristics of money. That is, cryptocurrencies don't simultaneously provide a medium of exchange, a store of value and a unit of account. This is due to their (often) severe volatility and price fluctuations. Libra's stable coin design provides the necessary stability, as it could be valued based on a basket of traditional securities and currencies.

Libra then had the potential to become a universally accepted global currency, it has the use base and the stability required to do so. Of course, it is not only Facebook planning its own currency. JP Morgan has an internal cryptocurrency, many other global investment banks are planning their own currency to launch in 2020, other large may be doing the same, and before long we would expect the big global tech firms to join in the cryptocurrency frenzy.

It is important for our analysis of the future of work that corporate cryptocurrencies have (at least initially) stability built into them. In order for them to replace money in (at least) some areas people need them to fulfil the functions of money. People need to have faith when accepting these for the payment of goods or services, such that the payment will be worth roughly tomorrow what it is worth today. People need to have confidence when saving corporate cryptocurrencies for their future, such that when the future is here, their savings will be worth around what they expect. Finally, people need to know that when they issue a bill and receive payment, the value they requested has not devalued in the intervening time. Sovereign currencies are hardly perfect in this regard, even 'stable' currencies like Pound Sterling. Geo-political events, standard inflation and government policy can erode the value of Pound Sterling over time, or practically instantly when considering key recent events such as quantitative easing, Brexit or Foreign Policy Announcements via Twitter. The initial cryptocurrencies such as Bitcoin do not provide this required stability. Corporate cryptocurrencies might, and if they can, have considerable implications.

> Perhaps the best indicator of this at the time of writing, Facebook is considered a AAA investment opportunity, the UK is considered a far riskier AA. Where would you put your money?

In contrast to the volatile supply and demand pricing mechanism of Bitcoin, Libra could maintain stability through backing based on a 'basket' of traditional currencies. However, the question arises of why should potentially AAA-rated Libra back itself with AA-rated GBP? Here is the crux of the argument: Libra's use base and stability plans could make it a currency de facto stronger, more reliable and flexible than Sterling or the US dollar. It comes as little surprise that the US House of Representatives response to Facebook's currency plans stated, 'these products may lend themselves to an entirely new global financial system that is based out of Switzerland and intended to rival US monetary Policy and the dollar', and the G7 stated that:

> They give rise to a number of serious risks related to public policy priorities including in particular, anti-money laundering and countering the financing of terrorism as well as consumer and data protection, cyber resilience, fair competition and tax compliance

'They could also pose issues related to monetary policy transmission, financial stability and the smooth functioning of public trust in the global payment system'. Additionally, they note that

> As large technology or financial firms could leverage vast existing customer bases to rapidly achieve a global footprint, it is imperative that authorities be vigilant in assessing risks and implications for the global financial system.

In short, 'The sovereignty of nations might be weakened or jeopardised by these new currencies', says Bruno Le Maire (French Finance Minister).

Cryptocurrency and Work

In its broadest sense, the idea of cryptocurrency is quite revolutionary; it has the potential to alter the relationship between the state and individual, alter the state power relationships and create a new-monetary system. The policy response around cryptocurrency is one of general confusion and complacency. If we consider the 'first' coins, of which Bitcoin is probably the most widely known, then its 'existence as a monetary substitute' is the key issue for the state. It is a market based, private asset which can be anonymous, replace sovereign currency in some circumstances and can provide a considerable (but not insurmountable) regulatory hill to climb.

Remember that the huge scale of Libra is staggering. Around half the global population may still become a customer of 'Facebook Bank'. This has considerable positive potential; a considerable proportion of these customers are at the moment of unbanked or underbanked and this project will provide basic financial services to millions. However, there is currently no institution to provide global oversight, and in the current age of increasing nationalism, protectionism and even isolationism, the political to create a global governing institution seems lacking.

Yet, Libra appears to have at least the potential and necessary characteristics to become a global currency. It has a formidable use base larger than any other global financial institution. It has the required stability to fulfil the characteristics of money. It even has a deposit protection scheme similar to the UK's Financial Services Compensation Scheme where individuals are protected against loss from the collapse of their institution, or in Libra's case the hacking of calibra (the Libra wallet or middleman). Furthermore, it has similar protection against scams and frauds as you would find with your high-street traditional banks. Crucially, at the time of writing, Facebook also has links with 7 million advertisers and 90 million businesses, this is a cryptocurrency proposition which has everything needed to succeed and challenge sovereign currencies. Dirk A. Zetzsche, Ross P. Buckley and Douglas Warner say:

> Libra could be a game changer. It signals the beginning of data giants entering into finance such a fundamental way as to have the potential, in poorer nations at least, to usurp many of the functions of the central bank, among others. Years ago, Mark Zuckerberg said, 'in a lot of ways Facebook is more like a government than a traditional company .... Libra is a wake-up call for all who have so far seen the data and financial economics as separate spheres.'

Libra is money by any standard definition other than the issuer. The Future of Working then has every possibility of including one or several global cryptocurrencies outside of state control and facilitating the new approach to work described in this book. To summarise global stable corporate, cryptocurrency provides organisations and workers to accept real time, infinitely divisible payments from anywhere in the world. Facebook is truly a global organisation potentially providing a currency outside the monetary policy of nation states. Workers could have a global profile capable of instantly accepting real-time payments from any organisations in the world.

CRYPTOCURRENCY AND THE STATE

A citizen will be able to pay for their goods and services via a mechanism outside of the state, a business will pay their costs and suppliers similarly. In fact, the state's intervention into this process via taxation or established processes of rates and charges, presents its only bastion or remaining beachhead in the economic system.

However, can a state collect taxes from an individual who is happy to accept electronic tokens for their own income? What is the taxable position? Let's assume that the transaction is similar to gold and the state taxes this at a rate equivalent to one who is paid in bullion; however, the value of bullion is historically stable, a cryptocurrency can transmute and the states' demands can become worthless on receipt. Gold has a value as it is relatively universally accepted, many cryptocurrencies have a specific and defined use, a state collecting tax in say Kodak Coin may glean extra value from small level exchanges for alternative currencies, including state currencies, but will ultimately have a need for considerable electronic photography processing.

Here, we get to the nub of the issue. Cryptocurrency is often designed and delivered at the level of the individual and the specific organisation, not at the level of the state. A state collecting tax at corporation level, must find a way to collect a medium which is not designed to be collated into a larger unit of account. Of course, one may query why the state does not simply tax activity even though it is conducted in an existing foreign currency. Why does the UK tax authority not simply tax activity conducted in cryptocurrency as activity conducted in say Euros? Taxing activity conducted in Euros is relatively easy. The state can assess the value of this activity in Pound Stirling and tax accordingly. As Euros are easily converted to Stirling, as are most of the major cryptocurrencies – although only at comparatively small amounts and this assumes that holders of Pound Stirling want cryptocurrency and vice versa. Taxes collected in cryptocurrency may well be unusable, taxes collected in Pound Stirling estimations of cryptocurrency activity are unreliable, both have no constancy in value and will be subject to continuous revaluation and adjustment.

Taxation issues aside however, here we are exploring a potential removal of the state from (at least part of) the economic process. Citizens will still require the provision of public goods, but the state will be removed from an individual's economic activity. Partially, we may be considering a technological barter process where there is activity and reward, but no tangible value created. For instance, an individual may earn a cryptocurrency reward for promoting a company on social media, this cryptocurrency reward may be redeemed for additional online memory. This activity would have previously been transacted by traditional currency, but where now is the involvement of the state?

One may imagine that the state will require stable digital stores of value, master digital currencies which will facilitate exchange between developing, corporate or even ad hoc digital currencies and state currency. This may facilitate the states continued involvement in the economic process, but would require a collaboration between the stateless and unconstrained master currencies, for example, Bitcoin and the state. The government would in essence have to agree a fixed exchange rate between a master cryptocurrency and Pound Stirling, which in turn would have floating exchange rates with all launched cryptocurrencies. Yet, clearly, this relationship is anathema to the notion of stateless cryptocurrencies, which are strengthened and increasingly valued by their users as vehicles of currency and commodity outside the control of the state.

We suggest that activity and value derived from cryptocurrency may be lessened with state involvement, transactions cannot be valued and activity will not necessarily occur within the constraints of regulation and state approval. Indeed, the notion of a state-supported cryptocurrency is at odds with the idea of a stateless digital currency.

The state may of course wish to consider if cryptocurrency is a long-term shift in its relations with the economy or perhaps a short-term phenomenon or even simply a speculative asset price bubble. We contest that even though there are elements, indeed classic bubble-like behaviour in individual cryptocurrencies indicative of a short-term interest and excitement will collapse. A driver of interest, investment and uptake of cryptocurrencies rather than the interest in any particular cryptocurrency is demonstrative of a societal shift towards a stateless mindset, potentially the end stages of the lessening of the nation states power as it is composed of individuals whose identity is centred in the online world. Indeed, for these truly global individuals whose friends, relationships, work, hobbies and education span numerous nation states and are seamlessly connected online in a way unimaginable even half a decade previously, a truly global online currency has numerous advantages above state-issued currency outside of simple speculation. This is a key driver of the uptake of cryptocurrency, there are no boarders and no exchange rates in an online world. A unit of cryptocurrency will in essence purchase the same amount of goods regardless of the holder's geography.

We of course accept that potentially even a large portion of the uptake and investment in cryptocurrency has been the result of speculation for sovereign currency return. This we contend is alien to the notion of a shift to cryptocurrency measured in terms of state and citizen power, but akin to speculative bubbles through history.

A speculative bubble is easy to call and difficult to prove. What are the drivers, is it irrational exuberance, misplaced optimism or the culmination of individual rational decisions into one collective mad rush. An individual firmly believing that the next individual will pay more for an investment, may be perfectly rational, our shop keepers, manufacturers and employers believe this on a daily basis. An individual investing in gold as they believe that someone in the future will pay more for it is rational, all individuals doing the same may lead to disaster.

'I can calculate the motion of heavenly bodies, but not the madness of people', supposed said by Sir Isaac Newton.

Here, we get to the nub. Throughout Western history, infrastructure expansion via new technology has taken the shape of a speculative bubble, albeit one with diminishing marginal returns for later entrants. If we consider historical bubbles as a point of analysis, then an individual railway company represents a new launch cryptocurrency, its shareholders then, users of the cryptocurrency and the goal to be the major railway company in the USA akin to the goal to be the default cryptocurrency, then we can draw some point of comparison and a notable end game. Individual railway companies came and went experiencing speculative bubbles, however the end goal was achieved, a connected United States utilising a new technology to improve the economic process. However, in the above, the state had at least implicit involvement in the process via its sovereign currency. Crypto-currency represents an entirely new relationship between the citizen and the economy excluding the state. Individual cryptocurrencies will stand or fall, however, the move towards a new transactional process may well result in a highly connected, transparent and efficient economic process. Similarly to how the railway diminished the power of local governments in favour of national, cryptocurrency may diminish the power of the nation state in favour of the global online hyper-economy.

THE CONVERGENCE OF ABC, A BRAVE NEW WORLD

The previous sections have explored the vast potential of these new technologies, that is, we have considered the individual effects of ABCs on the future of work and the worker. However, we argue that the convergence of these technologies into an approach, philosophy or if you will have a new way of work that has the potential to make tomorrow remarkably unlike today.

We will see in the following chapter that the existence and use of a new technology, even a generationally shifting one such as the web, isn't usually alone, able to fundamentally alter the existing order of things. Despite the following chapter's title, internet alone didn't kill the video store. The internet, electronic payment systems, numerous innovations in data transfer, storage, file formats crucially have a shift in the mindset of consumers along with a few key retail developments which killed the video store.

In this book, we consider that each of the components of ABC alone have the potential to, often significantly, alter the world of work, but it is the widespread potential of them operating together, and the increasing potential to design systems which incorporate all these technologies that has the ability to shift work and working away from our current understanding.

Crucially these 'supply-side' factors are in place; and a pessimistic, even dystopian view of the implementation of systems and processes by organisations with considerable power over the world of work and workers is possible, and certainly found in all manners of excellent science-fiction media. However, for us, at least part of this future has the potential to be bright. We argue that the implementation of the ABC triumvirate is not only survivable for the worker, but also has the ability to be beneficial for the organisation, worker and wider economy as well as having the innate ability to rebalance power between the workplace and worker.

Ultimately, the implementation of one aspect of the ABC triumvirate, that of Algorithms, has in many cases led to the increase in organisational power over the worker, the increase in precarity is well documented, extremely concerning and despite the best lobbying of the platforms themselves, rarely an add on, an extra cash job or a choice. Where it is these things, the freedom and flexibility is a great benefit, the student delivering on the weekend fills an economic need and earns extra cash, the middle-aged delivery with no choice but to survive on ad hoc uncertain and irregular work is in a different position. Choice is key, and the ability to choose this style of working instead of regular stable and secure work should be available; however, the removal of choice be making platform working the only option, demonstrates how power has shifted to the organisations. We would argue that the implementation of a new technology by an organisation will generally have that effect, why would a profit-making organisation implement a new technology, strategy or approach which reduces their power? This, we argue, is key, the ABC triumvirate represents a shift towards a new way of working, one that has a similarity with the platform precarity above, but one that via the incorporation of blockchain and cryptocurrency gives bargaining power to the individual worker. This is a shift in our idea of work to a world quite unrecognisable to the majority of workers. We term it *Bitwork*, and explain what we mean over the following chapters. It will require a reimagining of virtually every system we use for work, it will redefine notions of pay, reward and loyalty, ideas of the structure and existence of organisations and the economic laws of today may be just that, limited by the systems they seek to control, rather than the immutable omnipresent laws of natural science.

Therefore, what does the ABC triumvirate actually look like in practice? Many excellent books have explored the implementation of algorithms on the world of work, and earlier in this chapter we explore this and agree with the idea that where work can be split into sequences and processes algorithms and automation can generally do this and threatens human work. Additionally, through AI, machine learning and simple learning from experience, work which was previously considered outside the scope of algorithmic replication is coming under its consideration. Negotiation, creativity, academic research and a plethora of previously exclusively human activities, occupations and even vocations are, if not yet, soon to be under the algorithmic threat. For the A part then of the ABC triumvirate, we need to assume that, in probably less time than we'd like to assume, virtually every aspect of work is eventually able to be broken down to a system of processes.

The (B)lockchain part of the ABC is equally impactful, new ways of storing and accessing data are hugely important, but fall into insignificance against the philosophy and new ideas of data and service decentralisation. Blockchain could fundamentally transform services, manufacturing and even consumers' relationships with the products they purchase. Just like we can track the entire history of a single cryptocurrency, a consumer could be able to track the provenance of their products. It need not even be effortful. Simply a consumer could have specific ethical settings with their payment options, which will refuse payment (or reclaim payment) if their expected ethical conditions of production are not met. It is perfectly conceivable that promises around fair trade, ethical production or fair worker compensation could be unambiguously and effectively enforced, simply by a payment system obeying the customers' preference. For the B part then of the ABC triumvirate, we need to assume that, in the near future, all information has the option of being stored in a transparent, immutable and accessible manner, both facilitating the algorithmic process of A and providing instant real-time verification of contracts, promises and transfers. This is crucial for a Bitwork economy to develop and flourish.

The final (C)ryptocurrency aspect of the ABC, which potentially receives the most media attention for its role as an investment process, is a crucial component of the Bitwork economy. Earlier in this chapter we examined cryptocurrency and attempted to move away from its simple consideration as a new type of money or financial product to looking at the long-term implications of individuals and crucially corporations being able to issue their own currency The implications of this are simply staggering, the political, economic and social effects are yet to be explored, but what is virtually certain is that this will not be the last issuance of a corporate currency. For the C part of the ABC then, we'd like you to consider a (not too distant) future world of numerous competing corporate currencies, including sector currencies. We think it likely that where we have sectors with small numbers of large firms, trade bodies and representative groups will create sector coins; in the UK, for instance, we consider that an individual University is incapable of creating a competitive currency externally (they may, and many do create their own internal currencies for students to purchase to use around campus, etc.). However, it looks likely that a UK Universities coin would have enough users (staff and students) and asset backing to be competitive. (C) then represents a world where there are numerous, real time and infinitely divisible, stable pay and reward options.

The ABC then represents a world where virtually all work is broken down to sequences and processes, information is instantly verifiable and real time and infinitely divisible payment options are readily available (Fig. 1).

The next chapters of this book examines the implications for work and the worker of an economy where, facilitated by the ABC, work can be broken down to increasingly smaller processes, real time any value payments are possible

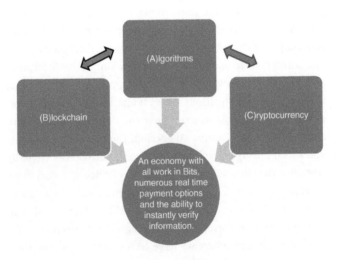

Fig. 1. The ABC and the Economy it Generates.

and both work done and payment received can be instantly and accurately verified. For the rest of the book, we will term this economy the 'ABC economy' and examine how it not only has the possibility of changing work completely, but how it is likely to do so. We propose that the ABC economy will eventually result in a new type of work which we term Bitwork and a new type of worker which we term the Bitworker. The rest of this book examines what this will look like on the level of the individual worker, the organisation and the wider economy and proposes how this could be beneficial for all and potentially rebalances power back towards the worker. Of course however, there are winners and losers and the discussions around choice from earlier should be remembered. Numerous policy prescriptions, which will be briefly considered in the later chapters, will also need to be enacted to harness the wider societal benefits of Bitworking, and governments worldwide will need to act in concert to realise the potential of this new philosophy of work.

Recap Definitions

The ABC economy – 'An economy with all work in Bits, numerous real-time payment options and the ability to instantly verify and trust information.'

Bitwork – 'The completion of a portion of an output or task in return for real-time precise payment'.

Bitworker – 'One who completes a portion of an output or task in return for real-time precise payment and generates their income from numerous organisations and in numerous forms'.

CONCLUSION

This initial chapter has described how ABC each individually have the potential to alter the world of work, but it is the convergence and interrelationship between these three technologies which generate what we term the ABC economy.

The ABC economy is an economy where all work is broken down to its component of process and sequences, which with AI and machine learning are further broken down to the fundamental processes. These processes are further broken down, the less specialism and skill required to do each individual one. The ABC economy has the mechanism and infrastructure for instantly verifiable information, and organisations have their own or alliance corporate currencies which remove geographic and international frictions and support the process to further break down work. This economy is a dynamic one, the incorporation of AI and machine learning approaches improve with every iteration of new data generated in the ABC economy. The progress towards this is exponential rather than linear and will begin to impact the world of work in the near future.

The logical outcome of this impact will be economic activity comprised mostly, of what we term Bitwork, but what is less certain is the outcome which we argue is generally beneficial. In the coming chapters, we will explore a beneficial scenario but also note the points where the dystopia of science fiction could come closer to reality.

2

INTERNET KILLED THE VIDEO STORE: LESSONS FROM HISTORY REPEATED IN THE BLOCKCHAIN WORLD?

INTRODUCTION

This chapter compares the history of the internet and its effect and destruction of firms and industries with the effects of a blockchain-enabled world and the convergence of tech in to one Organisation for Economic Co-operation and Development (OECD).

WILL THIS BE AS BIG AS THE INTERNET?

The history of the internet and its effect upon businesses and the world of work is relatively short but significant in the context of global economic development. The previous two decades has seen the birth of the gig economy and the disruption of existing business models to the detriment and elimination of some (Blockbuster video), compared to the creation of a new wave of platform businesses that include everything from Uber to Airbnb and Amazon.[1]

The disruption of the internet as a driving force for change has arguably been pervasive across all sectors and geographies changing the way that businesses promote their offerings and how we the consumer purchase their wares. Unsurprisingly, this technological pivot has impacted not just employers but crucially how we the workers are engaged and are remunerated in the modern world.

Gone is the expectation of a 'job for life' enjoyed by former generations, replaced by an expectation of constant change and the need to reinvent oneself decade to decade (or indeed far more frequently), both from the perspectives of the organisation and the individual. This enhanced churn of business model design and stylised worker has put pressure upon investment cycles and the skill sets of workers as the relentless pace of change has increased over recent times.

Moreover, in an increasingly globalised and interconnected world, the principles of comparative advantage have never held more true, as the pendulum of most efficient producer swings from nation to nation and region to region at an increasing pace. Such global shifts are acknowledged to be attributed to differences in factor conditions such as capital, labour and land availability as well as technological innovation, political and economic ideology and entrepreneurship. Such dynamism in the external environment is largely beyond the control and influence of individual workers. Furthermore, the ability of both current and future workers to predict the skill requirements a generation or more into the future is difficult, if not impossible, placing evermore pressure and uncertainty upon the decisions of current workers and the future 'Bitworkers'.

Such difficulties have been recognised by the Bank of England, who explain that 15 million UK jobs may be at risk to automation, whereas the Big 4 Firm PricewaterhouseCoopers predicts that 30% of UK jobs are potentially vulnerable.

Similarly, the University of Oxford identified 12 professions which have a 99% probability of being automated in their Future of Employment study by Frey and Osborne (2017) which is discussed later in this book, namely:

- Data Entry Keyers
- Library Technicians
- New Accounts Clerks
- Photographic Process Workers and Processing Machine Operators
- Tax Preparers
- Cargo and Freight Agents
- Watch Repairers
- Insurance Underwriters
- Mathematical Technicians
- Hand Sewers
- Title Examiners, Abstractors and Searchers
- Telemarketers.

In contrast, the same study identified the following professions as being least likely to be replaced by automation, with a probability of 0.35% or less for each profession to be replaced by automation. They are:

- Recreational Therapists
- First-Line Supervisors of Mechanics, Installers and Repairers
- Emergency Management Directors
- Mental Health and Substance Abuse Social Workers

- Audiologists
- Occupational Therapists
- Orthotists and Prosthetists
- Healthcare Social Workers.

Interestingly, the same study outlined a kind of barbell effect whereby the majority of professions were relatively safe from a probabilistic perspective but that the largest frequency of professions were either extremely safe or extremely likely to be replaced by automation and our algorithms, blockchain and cryptocurrencies (ABCs). If true, excessive observations at the extreme tails may further exacerbate the differences between the *haves* and the *have nots* potentially delivering aggregate benefit which is disproportionately received by the middle, upper and educated classes.[2] Such lists of disruption garner significant media headline attention but are difficult tools in isolation with which to better understand the changing nature of work and the role of the worker. However, what is clear is that disruptive change from automation is a supertrend that has rendered business models and workers as obsolete historically and is likely to continue to do so going forward.

We predict that a blockchain-enabled world discussed in the previous chapter is likely to exacerbate this *supertrend* still further. The combined economic superstorm of ABCs fosters a unique petri dish of economic conditions that will fracture business models still further, and therefore the future of work, at a rate much greater than that which we have struggled to cope with thus far.

But why should this be the case, and what is unique about these technological advancements that make this prediction valid in our opinion?

In short, this is a key component of the Fourth Industrial Revolution. To contextualise, we must always look back in order to look forward.

THE FOURTH INDUSTRIAL
REVOLUTION – INDUSTRY 4.0

The First Industrial Revolution was the shift away from human labour towards fossil fuels during the nineteenth century, shortly followed by the second, which was the amplification of these benefits by electrification and wired communication championed by forerunners such as Marconi. The creation of computers and digital systems in the latter half of the previous century represents the third, leaving us poised upon the precipice of the Fourth Revolution which is composed of our ABCs alongside that of Big Data, Artificial Intelligence and distributed financial systems (*DeFin*) and advancements in connectivity and cryptography, to name but a few.

Economic development has increased across these revolutions giving rise to a globalised and increasingly connected world which can be described as *hyper-globalised* with a weighting towards digital and capital intensive economies rather than the reliance upon labour across developed economies. Indeed, the World Economic Forum (2019) recently exclaimed that the Fourth Revolution is, 'more comprehensive and all-encompassing than anything we have ever seen'.

During these revolutions, we have witnessed the creation of ever larger organisations in an effort to reap scale benefits for investors and thus herding employees into increasingly larger pools of combined effort within their structures. Indeed, at the time of writing, some 15% of the S&P500 by market value is represented by just the largest 5 companies by market capitalisation, namely, Microsoft (4.22%), Apple (3.58%), Amazon (3.23%), Facebook (1.88%) and Warren Buffet's Berkshire Hathaway (1.69%).[3] This trend of growing market concentration, particularly amongst technology stocks, means that we now live in a world of more powerful lobbying upon the political classes of our nation states, and less so by industrial groups, but instead increasingly by individual organisations which are becoming all powerful. This observation further increases the likelihood of *regulator recapture* which was observed during the Financial Crisis 2007–2009, and represents a scenario where an industry begins to exert soft power influence over the very regulator that seeks to control it.

Our modern world is exemplified by multinationals such as McDonald's who now have a stronger credit rating than the country of Ireland, and the previously discussed Facebook behemoth, who, if they were a nation state generates annual profitability that would rank them 90th in the world by gross domestic product (GDP).

Therefore, what's next for this increasingly clumpy coagulation of human effort that is the globalised organisational form and its associated supply chains and diminished regulators?

THE SHORTENING OF SUPPLY CHAINS – ADD VALUE AND SPEED UP, OR DIE!

Advancements in blockchain have, and will, shorten the distance between consumer and businesses still further as the need for intermediaries diminishes and individuals is able to connect more easily with their upstream suppliers. Never has this more ably been exemplified than the case of Blockbuster video whose revenue declined from US$ 6 billion annual revenue to bankruptcy between 2004 and 2010. During the same period, Netflix increased from revenue near to US$ 2.2 billion, with latest revenue figures of just under US$ 16 billion in 2018, according to their statutory accounts.

At their peak in 2004, Blockbuster employed 84,300 people worldwide. In comparison, Netflix is currently generating aforementioned revenue more than three times larger with a workforce in 2017 of just 5,400 employees, as per their latest

Annual Report to shareholders. In summary, 3 times the revenue with 15 times fewer staff. Notwithstanding inflationary adjustments, revenue differentials not mirroring profit differentials and employee versus independent contractor mix variances between the competing businesses, it is clear that Netflix is a more efficient vehicle to deliver digital content.

Arguably, we the consumers have gained as we now have more choice and quality media content available on demand from organisations such as Netflix at monthly subscription rates not too dissimilar to the single overnight rental charges levied by Blockbuster and their like, not to mention the inconvenience of returning the physical video or DVD. So, if we the consumers have gained, alongside shareholders with the foresight to invest early, then who has lost?[4] Answer: the circa 80,000 net reduction in employed workers, not considering other alternative competitors to both businesses in their respective time periods.

The redeployment of the vast majority of such job losses must be absorbed by other industries with low-skill capacity otherwise national unemployment figures will begin to creep upwards. However, what we have observed in many countries is stable or declining unemployment coupled by a decrease in real wages thereby putting additional pressure upon low-income family earnings and consequently fostering populist movements which have been defined by Credit Suisse as an *Angry Society* supertrend. The London School of Economics observed exactly this where Pessoa and Reenan (2014, p. 10) highlighted that

> *basic economics suggests that workers' real hourly compensation should grow in line with GDP per hour worked over the long run. But between 1972 and 2010, US productivity grew by 84% while median wages only grew by 21%.*

Moving forward from such innovations, there are many who correctly explain that blockchain is just another type of database that is able to organise and write new entries for multiple users in real time. All true, and therefore a counter-argument suggests that similarly large-scale disruption owing to our ABCs and in particular Blockchain, may be over-hyped. However, such blockchain enhancements permit users to negate the need for a central arbiter, in a permissionless variant at least, thereby destroying not just supply chains of historical norms across industries but often the necessity for organisations at all.

Nowhere is this exhibited more keenly as the example of Bitcoin, the founding cryptocurrency which was theorised by the pseudo-anonymous Satoshi Nakomoto in 2008, with the first Bitcoins being created, or mined, in the *Genesis Block* on the 3rd of January the following year. Such technologies are *bank killers* permitting users to store and transact monetary value without the need for financial institutions. Individuals can now be their own banks, for better or worse, with the collective Bitcoin community administering control of the monetary system as a whole in terms of supply and technological protocols.

For Bitcoin, gone is the concept of a nation state. There are no shareholders or traditional governance structures. There is no tax domicile or directors or memorandum and articles of association which constitute the mechanics of how an organisation is run. Instead, we bear witness to a new type of pseudo-organisation, akin to the identity of its founder, which by virtue of its permissionless nature allows a wisdom of crowds' effect, not just to discover a higher truth, but rather to service our day to day needs without the need for a traditional centralised organisational form.

The above is a blockchain-enabled world which will shorten supply chains still further and in some cases, similar to that of Bitcoin, eliminate them completely. This is a technology that will render intermediaries which add insufficient value as obsolete, thereby allowing consumers and source suppliers to exchange goods and services over time and space with confidence contemporaneously.

Such exchanges of economic value leverage the tenants of: a shared ledger (a record), cryptography (verifiable movement of data between counterparties), a consensus protocol (agreed requirements to *do* business) and shared contracts (business terms and agreements). Importantly, this disruption is not just limited to financial services and banking but rather has applicability to any organisation or supply chain that holds or exchanges monetary value or information. Hence, many believe, including these authors, that blockchains have potential across all industry sectors and geographies with significant impact upon employers and the world of work.

THE DECENTRALISED INFORMATION ECONOMY

With this technologically enabled shift comes the consequent development of an information economy that will manifest the Fourth Industrial Revolution. An era where, in the case of organisations such as EnergiMine, individuals cannot now only be their own bank but can also, for example, generate surplus electricity in their homes and sell it directly to organisations who are willing to pay for it. This can be done via intermediaries such as The National Grid in the UK but instead using EnergiMine is done directly using a tokenised blockchain platform solution. Much more efficient and without a middle man who previously took a cut not always adding sufficient value to warrant that.

The above begs the question as to which organisational forms will be disrupted in such a way by blockchain advancements and the algorithms and cryptocurrencies which complement and wrap around this technology? As previously discussed, if an organisation either moves or holds data then such innovations are relevant and perhaps likely if not inevitable. For our money (excuse the pun), this represents all businesses where such data may be as varied as commercially valuable information such as biometrics of potential patients but extends just as easily to monetary data which may be in fiat, or indeed, cryptocurrency forms.

Such cryptocurrencies presently number at more than 2,000 according to coinmarketcap.com, with the majority running upon blockchain infrastructure systems which are decentralised by design. They represent the democratisation of money which is no longer tied to the monopoly of nation states but instead to the control of the crowd, or perhaps more interestingly to the design of a non-sovereign issuer such as Facebook's Libra currency or JP Morgan's JPM Coin. In fact, *The Financial Times* reported in June 2019 that no fewer than 13 global investment banks are planning to launch their own digital currencies by the end of 2020. It would seem that multinationals now appreciate the potential to not only sell goods and services to consumers but also to sell the monetary systems with which these can now be purchased. Watch this space.

When the technologies of blockchain and cryptocurrency are threatening the long established monopoly of monetary policy which has historically been dominated by central banks and governments, we must understand the significant potential for the disruption of traditional industrial structures across any sector or geography. Nowhere is immune.

This is not only limited to private enterprises such as Walmart who in 2019 filed a patent to use a digital currency to enable faster and cheaper transactions in their stores. State actors are also not slow to consider adoption in full or in part. New Zealand recently legalised the payment of salaries in cryptocurrency whilst The Bank of England published multiple research papers in 2018 exploring how a *central bank digital currency* (CDBC), or crypto pound in this instance, would work in the UK economy alongside the existing Great British Pound fiat currency equivalent.

However, it can be considered that such announcements by governments and central banks are far from endorsements of cryptocurrencies. Indeed, Izabella Kaminska of *The Financial Times* argued in August 2019 that in the case of New Zealand this was less of an endorsement and more guidance in terms of tax treatment. Employers and employees may have previously incorrectly observed income tax loopholes to exist when payment is made in non-fiat currency form. The New Zealand tax authorities have removed this misconception by insisting that 'pay as you earn' income tax is still due on such earnings whilst also maintaining that cryptocurrency 'is not money'.[5] A key lexicological point and one that we would be in agreement with.

Perhaps most poignantly, after five years of development, the People's Bank of China (PBOC) announced in August 2019 that it is ready to launch its own digital currency which similar to the UK's theorised CDBC is centralised in nature.[6] However, such examples of actual or potential state-level adoption of cryptocurrencies aid the overall diffusion of innovation for this new technology thereby encouraging other nations, corporates and individuals to do likewise. Indeed, since we came off the gold standard at various points in time during the latter half of the previous century, is our present fiat currency now not a construct of confidence? If such confidence can be championed by Governments then cryptocurrency and the blockchain technologies upon which they run may become *sticky*, in the words of the consultants and marketers. They are therefore more likely to creep into our expected norms in the future world of work. Crucially however, such actions represent the institutionalisation of cryptocurrencies which although making wider, if not complete, adoption more likely, comes with a price tag. The stateless and pseudo-anonymous nature of cryptocurrencies such as Bitcoin or Monero is not maintained, but rather a centralised, or permissioned, blockchain is employed allowing the state to see all and thereby mitigate the risk of tax avoidance and reduce the potential use and growth by the shadow economy.[7] Ironically, it can be argued that the adoption which cryptocurrency enthusiasts' desire requires some form of aforementioned state-level adoption or endorsement which is the very thing which some libertarians championed in early cryptocurrency forms – a non-sovereign currency to empower the individual.

Examples of such state-level innovations are now less of a hypothetical but rather are already operating, or are about to be so, in our economies. Oftentimes, financial services are focus for many but although readily applicable we must not limit our predictions to the application of ABCs to this sector, although it is perhaps understandable why we do so.

In the UK, for example, the Financial Services Conduct Authority (FCA) regulates permissioned activities within its jurisdiction. However, in recognition of the benefits of such technologies coupled with the inability of such advancements to fit the existing rules structure, they (the FCA) operate a Sandbox initiative. This system permits a quasi-regulated environment which allows organisations to push and bend rather than break the rules much to the success of its previous five cohorts of members thus far. To date, this initiative has seen innovative peer-to-peer lending platforms, blockchain-based real-time settlement systems, derivatives denominated in cryptocurrencies and predictive artificial intelligence credit-scoring systems. All of which are bleeding edge technologies with the potential to disrupt and thereby affect the future world of work with which this text is focussed.

CDBC

CBDCs are the possible scenario for the future of money alongside: permissionless cryptocurrencies, corporate-issued non-sovereign currency and the securitised self. Essentially, the differences between these competing forms are the identity of the issuer, namely, the central bank, a permissionless blockchain, a corporation or an individual.

CBDCs are an institutional response to the threat of alternative forms of future money to the current state monopolistic control over monetary policy. Largely theoretical at present, there is little practical evidence to support the case for CBDCs. The Bank of England published four research papers on CBDCs in 2018 which discussed how a crypto Great British Pound might work alongside the existing fiat currency GBP. This was envisaged over three alternative macroeconomic structures which differed by the availability of such a CBDC to alternative actors within the UK economy. Furthermore, The Bank also issued a number of questions to encourage interested parties to engage with, such as how a possible CBDC might be used as a monetary policy tool?

Further afield a number of other central banks are investigating this technology. Not least, is The PBOC who earlier in 2019 announced that they had been researching CBDCs for the previous five years, and that they find merit in their results and therefore aim to launch in 2020.

These next-generation monetary systems will have a direct impact upon the future world of work. Individual workers will be able to be remunerated and spend using our existing fiat currencies alongside their CBDC equivalents. The merits of each of these parallel systems are that a CBDC is effectively a tokenised fiat currency. It enables users to leverage the benefits of cryptocurrencies such as microtransactions, lower transaction costs, faster and more transparent transactions and the ability to store wealth on a Blockchain ledger rather than with a regulated centralised custodian. The key difference between CBDCs and permissionless cryptocurrencies such as Bitcoin is that such CBDCs would not be permissionless. Rather, they would be controlled in terms of their use and access and the transactions would not be anonymous or even pseudo-anonymous. This institutionalisation of cryptocurrency helps to mitigate the risks of money laundering thereby also satisfying national and global regulators in terms of Know Your Customer and Anti-Money Laundering cheques. Perhaps more importantly, such CBDCs would also defend the state from a reduction in tax take caused by individuals being remunerated in new forms of future money where their taxable gains and income can be sheltered from the tax system, a collection of activities known as the shadow economy.

A global survey by The Bank of International Settlements, the bank for central banks, showed that 70% of central banks worldwide are exploring CBDCs. This statistics was based upon 63 responses and is therefore a clear indication of this increasingly important development in the 'C' of our ABC triumvirate. A useful current summary of CBDC's was provided by Tokenomy (2019).[8]

ENTER THE ALGORITHMS TO STEAL AWAY YOUR ROUTINE JOB

Going forward, we see algorithms and the growth of AI combining to drive change for the world of work through the disruption of business models, employers and workers alike. For example, the emergence of algorithmically controlled robo-advisors in the field of financial services aims to standardise much of the early-stage consumer experience as well as

removing significant layers of low- to mid-level skilled workers from organisational cost structures, which can be passed
on to consumers in the form of lower fees. Examples of such
robo-advisors include Betterment LLC and Personal Capital
who boasted $13.5 billion and $8.5 billion of assets under
management as at February 2019, respectively, according to
Sean Allocca of www.financial-planning.com (2019). However, such benefits are felt far beyond the world of finance,
including smart personal assistants such as Siri, Cortana and
Google Now, along with security surveillance through the
personalisation of news feeds and optimisation of farming
yields and crop harvest strategic planning based upon real-
time pollination data obtained by drones.

An exciting future with significant value added potential
for industry either through the enhancement of products and
services or through the ability to offer the same goods and services cheaply. For the world of work, this is of course a double-
edged sword. For the worker, requiring not just the basic and
advanced skills and training of the past but now a dynamic
cross-functional skill set to adapt in the present as well as for
the duration of their future careers. The rising need for the
polymath who can be dynamic perhaps across multiple industries will not necessarily become the norm but will certainly
play a larger part as such competing demands and changes are
made to our previously safe haven industries which up until a
generation past delivered a now fabled job for life.

Such cross-functional skills are defined in the O*NET
Content Model published by The World Economic Forum in
2016 as; *cognitive abilities*, *physical abilities*, *content skills*
and *process skills*. It is these *abilities* of the first two categories which are higher order and difficult to imitate, often
drawing upon subjective or creative aspects of our human
acumen. For example, we can apply these to the legal industry
where the profession and coders of smart contracts, hosted

on blockchains such as Ethereum, are combining their efforts and coming to the fore.[9]

The ability to automate much of the routine, but often highly billable operations, of the legal profession has the potential to reduce costs and execution times considerably. Self executing wills, conveyance contracts, trust funds and insurance payments have all been theorised and implemented. For example, AXA Global recently developed an oracle to monitor global flight delays in real time in order to administer payments for their travel insurance and also better price their future products as an underwriting service.[10]

Nonetheless, such examples are reasonably vanilla in nature and although represent a threat to the legal industry they are unlikely to negate their need completely. Indeed, how could we possibly hope to codify within smart contracts concepts in law such as 'best efforts' and 'reasonableness'? Some argue that with advancements in AI even challenges such as these may one day be achievable. However, the worker of today need caution against the threat to largely routine and overpriced activity roles which are ripe for technological disruption as opposed to the aforementioned higher order abilities. Not to be flippant of this disparity, such non-uniform disruption across the skill-level continuum that is our modern workforce will have a disproportionate detrimental impact upon different demographics by country, social class and education. A worrying hypothesis that is aligned with the findings of the previously discussed study by Frey and Osborne (2017) of the University of Oxford.

Indeed, what happened to the aforementioned employees who previously worked at Blockbuster Video? A net loss of some 80,000 jobs globally, comparing Blockbuster's demise directly with the emergence of Netflix.

Similar to the now defunct or heavily depleted employing industries, the detrimental effect on the workforce is not evenly distributed but rather is concentrated both geographically and demographically. The (in)/ability of workers to retrain coupled with a sharp loss of opportunity and perhaps local public funding too can lead to whole towns, cities and even regions suffering for a generation or more, for example, coal mining and shipbuilding in the UK.

The invisible hand of globalisation is quick to reward labour and capital efficiencies but is remorseless in punishing no longer viable employment without state intervention, which is often unsustainable in the longer term in the face of technological change. Many such disrupted workers were forced in to lower skilled and consequently lower paid service industries such as the much maligned modern call centres which have drawn comparison to the working mills of the Industrial Revolution.

However, the distinction with our disruptive ABCs is not one of incremental change but rather a paradigm shift in our perceptions of a worker and their relationship with their employer(s). The culmination of algorithms, machine learning and AI will further fragment the activities of the worker into increasingly narrow microtasks which can then be efficiently and automatically allocated to the individuals. This is effectively what has happened with organisations such as Uber which connects suppliers and consumers within their platform thereby driving down price and increasing competition.

Much of this value adding, or arguably worker destroying activity, has had the effect in recent years of removing protections for workers as well as in some cases driving down aggregate household incomes thereby necessitating legislation for minimum wages and minimum living wages alike.

This rise of the *gig economy* over the previous decade or so has further disintermediated the full-time employment contract which previously gave the worker future income surety. Such fragmentation of the traditional organisational form and overall worker rights may point to ABCs as a detrimental cause but ironically may also look to blockchain for a protective solution, a Blockchain-based Trade Union Movement.

BLOCKCHAIN AS A CAUSE AND SOLUTION? THE BIRTH OF THE *DIGITAL COOPERATIVE* OR *DCOP*

Trade union membership has been steadily falling in many developed economies over the previous 20 years. Since 1998, total membership has fallen by approximately: 0.5 million in the UK, 0.3 million in the Netherlands, 2 million in Japan, and 0.2 million in Austria according to the latest OECD numbers. To contextualise the longer-term trend, some 30% of wage and salaried workers were trade union members in the USA at the end of the Second World War compared with just 12% in 2010 at the conclusion of the Financial Crisis. A more rapid decline in membership was observed in Australia which declined from circa 40% in 1992 to just 20% in 2011.

There are many reasons to explain this movement not least the explosion of personal debt and house prices (and therefore mortgage debt) over a similar period. Bluntly, debt disciplines labour and therefore a worker who is carrying more debt has less financial freedom and flexibility to engage in strike action, or similar.

Presently, according to the Bureau of Labor Statistics, almost 10% of workers in the USA are engaged on a non-employed basis. They are categorised as: independent contractors (6.9%), on call workers (1.7%), temporary help agency workers (0.9%) and workers provided by contract firms (0.6%). With 1 in 10 workers now being a contract worker this poses challenges for the individual worker who is now absorbing the risks and rewards of individual employment at an increasing rate. Couple this with the previously discussed historical decrease in trade union membership along with the potential impact of the ABCs of our triumvirate and we may reasonably expect a larger proportion of our future workforce to be classified as such contractors who will not only carry more risk but will also garner less trade union type protections at exactly the time when they perhaps need them.

With writers such as Brian Rashid predicting *The Rise of The Freelancer Economy* in *Forbes* Magazine in 2017, we might anticipate not just an increase in absolute worker numbers in the *gig economy* but also the emergence of the *Bitworker* who is a microtask contractor enabled by the technology of our ABCs. See later chapters for more discussion of this.

If true, such predictions will place increased pressures upon the individual worker although this will be traded-off against enhanced flexibility and choice but is often typified by lower real wages despite aggregate improvements in national unemployment numbers. Such workers will bear increased risk and responsibility for: sickness, holidays, pension contributions, taxation and the provision of work being made available to them. However, historically, it has been the pooling of such risks with other similar individuals which has been a viable strategy in alleviating the pressures and haphazard circumstance for any single individual. The very concept of insurance, and something which trade union membership can, and did, previously protect on behalf of workers (members) who had need of it.

The transparency and sharing of information and value may one day allow such Bitworkers to pool their risks and rewards similar to that of a cooperative type model, which here we have termed a *digital cooperative* or DCOP.[11]

A DCOP could be a permissioned blockchain system through which Bitworkers pool their collective efforts, receive payment and perhaps even bill and receive payment through, either in fiat or cryptocurrency monetary form. In doing so, such a blockchain system could levy a commission/an annual charge upon its members which would be visible by all. These aggregate fees would be used to cover administrative costs as well as validated predetermined conditions of need by members including: sickness pay, maternity pay or lack of available work support. The proposed DCOPs are not too dissimilar to the original Livery Companies of the City of London which originated in the twelfth century and are composed of merchant guilds and trade associations, including but not limited to: The Goldsmiths, The Grocers, The Masons and more recently the Honourable Company of Airpilots.[12]

Their original purpose was one of maintaining quality, lobbying government and charitable efforts. However, although DCOPs could form around particular trades and professional disciplines similar to that of the merchant guilds it is likely that their formation would be more orchestrated around risk pooling to overcome the drawbacks of a Bitworker relative to an equivalent employed person.

Extending this thinking further, we could perhaps see DCOPs with a global reach composed of many millions of workers, some of whom may choose multiple DCOP memberships through which to channel their multiple income streams. Indeed, such aggregation of worker effort enabled by Blockchain technology may be a natural response to the increasing concentration of corporate power to the detriment of worker rights and remuneration.

Finally, how would member status such as sickness, maternity or lack of work be validated in such an automated blockchain system? In full, or in part, by Oracles who can access other external systems to validate such occurrences for individual members and thereby remunerate them with the surplus funds of the DCOP in line with the predefined arrangement terms.

TOO BIG TO REGULATE?

Beyond the writing of Andrew Sorkin's (2009) *Too Big to Fail* analogy, we see a continued trend of hyper-globalisation where multinationals increasingly rival the regulatory and legal powers of the nation state by virtue of their size, lobbying power and ability to trade nations off against one another in order to maximise their own returns. An entirely rational and optimum strategy for any corporate, and for which the danger to the wider economy became apparent during the last financial crisis.

The ability of corporates to issue their own non-sovereign corporate currencies goes someway to furthering this cause which when combined with blockchain technology and the algorithms and AI of the remaining *triumvirate* have the potential to further shift power away from nation states and their citizens further in favour of such corporates.

However, this is not a foregone conclusion to a dystopian end. Although larger than ever before such leviathan organisations are presently not too big to regulate. For example, in January 1984, AT&T was broken up into AT&T long distance company, as we know it today, along with a further seven Regional Bell Operating Companies which represented the local phone networks in the USA. The foresight of the US Government along with Judge Harold Green who presided over the decision in 1982, was instrumental in recognising that the dominance of AT&T for the majority of the twentieth century in controlling much of US telecommunications infrastructure was not only bad for competition and therefore prices but that the technology was increasingly becoming a pervasive and an integral part of the country's economy from which all businesses and citizens relied. Yet this foresight perhaps fades when considering the growth of these constituent parts into entities again, perhaps, too big to fail.

However, in the modern world, we have observed the development of platform businesses such as Facebook (connecting content consumers with advertisers), Airbnb (Available accommodation providers with accommodation seekers), Amazon (Buyers with sellers) and Netflix (Film producers with viewers). Market and profit concentration continues to further corral to these largest of new multinationals much to the expense of their workers, such as Facebook who employ tens of thousands of contract workers who lack the remuneration and working conditions of their employed counterparts, according to Bloomberg (2019). Their roles range from bus drivers to content moderators which although 'crucial' according to Facebook are only recently being afforded a minimum pay rise from $15 to $20 per hour in certain regions within the USA, much to the maligned response from some such workers who have declared that 'contractors are people too!'

With Facebook's 2019 announcement of the structure of their Libra coin, the march towards profit maximisation at the expense of some workers may be further enhanced as employees are initially to be able to receive up to 25% of their salary in the Libra coin, should they so wish. That is only a very short step away from a much higher percentage and perhaps even a mandatory remunerating currency. If you want to work here then we pay you in our currency. Almost an employee share scheme on steroids! In the wake of recent data scandals, choosing your Social Media as your bank and by extension your monetary system is perhaps a step too far for many in terms of their ability to trust any particular organisation. Moreover, the quasi-decentralised structure of, say, the proposed Libra currency may lead many to suggest that it is not a true cryptocurrency as it is not fully decentralised and permissionless in comparison to the control of Libra by The Libra Council which is composed of Facebook along with 28 of their original partner organisations.[13]

The private nature of employment contracts between employees and their employer entitles them to make arrangements for a variety of forms of emoluments that are conducive to both parties. They can include: salary, bonus, pension contributions, company car, stock options, vouchers and private medical insurance to name but a few. All of the above are permitted in the majority of nations globally, and in the UK are allowable forms of taxable income as recognised by HMRC (Her Majesty's Revenue & Customs) and under The Employment Rights Act 1996. The extension of this list to include cryptocurrencies issued and controlled by the employer is akin to company scrip or tokens whereby an employee can only spend their salary with their own employer. Such actions curtail the freedom of the individual and had therefore fallen out of favour during recent centuries with many nations outlawing the payment of salaries in anything other than state-recognised currency.[14]

Nonetheless, although under threat, the power of nation states and workers alike is not emasculated. In July of 2019, the French Government led by President Macron approved the French Digital Services Tax which represents a 3% tax on revenue generated in France by large, and mainly US large technology firms such as Google and Microsoft, much to the frustration of the US Government. Critically, the tax is on revenue rather than profit thereby mitigating the risk of profit manipulation by transfer pricing strategies. Such policies evidence that a brake is still possible on the supertrend of hyper-globalisation and in particular the technology firms that are likely to more readily leverage the triumvirate that is our ABCs.

In a world of low rates and yields alongside geopolitical shocks, and the aforementioned rise of populism, the emergence of such corporate currencies may represent a relatively safe harbour where citizens and workers of the world can diversify their comparatively limited wealth against external foreign currency exchange rate risks and shocks. Such a strategy has previously only been afforded to institutional and high net worth investors but obviously poses a risk to the monetary policies of central banks and nation states alike should their workers begin to choose to be remunerated in the currency of their employer, or even that of a rival nation state.

Presently, the much hyped emergence of such corporate coins should be evaluated in the context Roy Amara's Law (1983) which states that with the emergence of new disruptive technologies we tend to overestimate their short-term impact but conversely underestimate their medium to long-term impact. With as yet undefined timescales for the impact of the triumvirate and the Fourth Industrial Revolution, it is difficult to ascertain our location on this over/under-hyped analogy. However, aligned with the other commentators, organisations such as Credit Suisse hosted a conference in Singapore in April 2019 with a panel discussion entitled 'Blockchain – revolutionary or overhyped?' Such thinking might suggest that we are presently in, or exiting, the early overhyped stage according to Roy Amara. Our task now is to envisage the potential future scenarios for the world of work, particularly those second-order effects which are often the most disruptive. Akin to the fax machine industry which responded to the innovation of email and the internet with an internet ready fax machine, the first-order effect or reaction, which is much less important than the macro-detrimental impact to the wider fax machine industry over the medium to long term.

CONCLUSION

Overall, in this chapter, we have reflected upon the disruptive impact of the internet through the case study of the demise of

Blockbuster alongside the emergence of Netflix after the turn of the millennium through to the present day. We explored the consequential impact upon jobs in aggregate from this case as well as outlining professions which are likely to be replaced by automation whilst looking forward to how this could be exacerbated further by the enabling technologies that are our ABCs in the context of the Fourth Industrial Revolution.

Furthermore, we outlined the *supertrend* of shortening supply chains, the institutionalisation of cryptocurrencies citing global examples and how this is likely to affect the worker of tomorrow, for example, worker remuneration in corporate coin. Importantly, the predicted decentralised cooperative, or digital decentralised cooperative (DCOP), blockchain organisational form was defined and justified in response to the above changes which may better support the management of new risks and multiple income streams for the worker of tomorrow which is discussed in more detail in the next chapter.

NOTES

1. A *platform business* is an enterprise that connects users in exchange for profit extraction often using technology to deliver a place where such connections take place. Examples include: Netflix (producers and consumers of media content), Facebook (advertisers with consumers of advertising and social experiences), Airbnb (landlords with prospective short-term tenants) and Uber (willing and available drivers with users who wish to undertake a journey).

2. The global Geni Coefficient has increased from 0.5 to 0.65 between 1820 and 2008. With significant increases noted in the UK, US and Sweden since the 1980s, whilst France and Germany have remained relatively static. Note that the Geni Coefficient is a statistical measure of inequality where a figure of 1.0 equals perfect inequality and figure of 0.0 represents perfect equality.

3. Market capitalisation is the number of adjusted *free float* shares available multiplied by the share price. This calculation is the sum product of all publically available, or listed, shares, for example, Facebook Class A and B ordinary shares on the American Stock Exchange (NASDAQ). Such dual-class structures are becoming increasingly more prominent in contravention of the *one share one vote* principle.

4. Since Netflix's Initial Public Offering (IPO) was initiated in May 2002, their stock has increased from US$ 1.21 to US$ 343.28 at the end of May 2019, some 17 years later. This represents a 139% average compound annual growth rate; not too shabby during a period of *lower for longer* yields. A clear example of how economic value can shift between competing business models (from the old to the new) owing to technological disruption.

5. Global tax authorities including New Zealand in 2019 and the UK in 2018 have ruled that if cryptocurrency payments are regular to employees and an active market exists where employees can 'cash out' to fiat currency then the income tax treatment is no different to that of fiat currency remuneration.

6. At the time of writing, no fixed launch date has been announced by the PBOC.

7. Unlike Bitcoin, Monero is actually cryptographically dark and is deigned to maintain complete anonymity. It is presently ranked as 10th by coinmarketcap.com with a market capitalisation of US$ 1.45 billion. Its uses are often championed by criminals, tax evasion strategists and libertarians. However, we should maintain balance in our comparison to existing fiat currencies which are not immune from such criminal use. In fact, Europol welcomed the decision of The European Central Bank in 2016 to stop printing €500 notes which alarmingly represented 30 percent of monetary circulation by value and yet most European citizens had never seen one let alone used one leading many to infer that their use for criminal purposes such as money laundering was likely.

8. See the table on current CBDCs in Tokenomy (2019).

9. The term 'smart contract' was originally coined by Nick Szabo in 1994 as 'a piece of code that executes the terms of a contract on its own'.

10. An oracle is AI often embedded within a smart contract to observe future external events in order to then allow the underlying contract to decide whether a particular action should be taken.

11. A cooperative is an organisation that is owned by the members who are the purchasers and consumers of the goods and services which the organisation creates. They are a not-for-profit entity whose raison d'etre is the fulfilment and betterment of their members.

12. In all, 110 organisations have existed within this umbrella structure since its inception.

13. Note that in October 2019, 7 of the 28 founding Libra members withdrew from the project including Mastercard, Visa and Stripe. Public statements were neutral by explanation but political and regulatory pressures were brought to bear upon the core businesses of these founders by virtue of their previous membership in this project.

14. Measures passed by the British Parliament in the 19th century regarding the method of payment of wages. Certain employers paid their workmen in goods or in tokens, which could be exchanged only at shops owned by the employers – the so-called truck system. The Truck Act of 1831 listed many trades in which payment of wages must be made in coins. It was amended by an Act of 1887, which extended its provisions to cover virtually all manual workers. Source: www.oxfordreference.com (2019). Accessed on 25 November 2019.

3

JOB 1/JOB 2/JOB 3 ... JOB *n*

INTRODUCTION

In this chapter, we discuss the effect of algorithms, blockchain and cryptocurrency (ABC) on the individual, with a focus on the idea of multiple roles, multiple income sources (in multiple coins) and implications for loyalty and retirement and so on. Self-employment on a massive scale is hypothesised and how that may manifest itself across our economies and society as a whole.

ABC WILL (EVENTUALLY) TRANSFORM WORK INTO MICROTASKS

In Chapter 1, we postulated that the ABC economy would continue the current breakdown of work into its component parts, and then those into their fundamentals and so on. Artificial Intelligence (AI) and machine learning approaches will be key to this, as with each process successfully completed by numerous different actors, the data generated will allow refinement and increased specialisation.

For examining the notion of the Bitworker, we postulate that this continued refinement of work processes will result in a small number of types of work, classified by the necessary Bitworker types to do them rather than their specific tasks and roles.

For instance, there may well exist four types of work once the fundamental process of economic activity has been unveiled (Table 1).

Of course, these will be continually refined by the ABC. We have 'guessed' at this refinement to two points above. Under creative, we have 'Provide the initial start point for creative algorithms' and under technical we have 'Provide insight on subjectivity', both of these (potentially microtasks) have the potential to cross the types and workers highly skilled in these areas could thrive in the above framework.

There are numerous activities which we can just begin to guess at and only note ongoing trends – we are unsure of how people will adapt and how far they will allow the ABC to refine and replace. However, we do note that the UK government is about to begin a trial of Alexa for making GP appointments, that algorithms are 'advising' on sentences and the chances of reoffending, and that robotic financial advice is fast becoming a trusted option.

Table 1. Themes of Microtasks.

Physical	Creative	Technical	People-based
Physical labour too complex, bespoke or expensive for a machine to do	Compose music	Fix spaghetti code	Support carer automation
Freight, delivery to unconnected (off chain) regions	Provide the initial start point for creative algorithms	Manually debug	Childcare
	Marketing	Provide insight on subjectivity	Teaching and healthcare

Case Study – The Increase of Tech in Our Lives

It is an undeniable fact that technology has continued its presence in our lives, to an extent where those not integrated online with a digital footprint, often create suspicion with authorities. Recently, the media have discussed cases where individuals anxious to maintain low or zero online presence, have been refused credit, mortgages or state services. Clearly, the more telling aspect of the infiltration of technology into our everyday lives, is how we access even the most basic and straightforward services in the UK. Most local authority recycling and waste services have online as their preferred access route (they generally provide a telephone service which is often expensive inefficient and under resourced, meaning in practice, online is the only feasible access option). Bank branches continue to close apace with the majority of banking services, particularly outside cities and large towns, are only available online. Your local doctors may offer appointments online and those unable to make online appointments call and wait for an appointment with far less options and support. Utility services provide cheaper options for people who use online meter readings, account checking, etc. and HMRC's self-assessment service allows an online submission three months later than a paper-based one. The vast majority of university courses are online supported and the vast majority of additional training support in adult education is found online complementing the large-scale withdrawal locally, on a face-to-face format. Of course, political ideology coupled with the technological developments has generated a shift towards what is seen as (often incorrectly) a more cost-effective online service approach. The move towards everything online has efficiencies, cost savings and benefits to the customer and to the organisation; however, this is not a universal shift. Many sectors of society either through demographic reasons cost reasons simple geographic regions people to participate and the question for this book is what happens to this aspect of the workforce if and when the majority of work moves online. We can see even now in the world of work that jobseekers who whether for demographic or financial reasons are not online can only access online services on an ad hoc non-continual basis say via a local library, lose out in the job market to jobseekers who are continually online.

This idea of being continually online, of having a constant online presence is a key point in this book, quite simply workers in the ABC economy will generally be constantly online. This idea however is particularly similar to how a seemingly increasingly number of people already live their lives through their mobile phone, their integration with social media, their receipt of news and the ordering of their lives. AI assistance, present in smart speakers and smart phones, is increasingly managing our diaries and activities, and it is not a large stretch of the imagination to consider in the future the AI assistance on your phone which monitors your emails, your events, your activities to arrange your calendar for you will do the same with incoming microtasks.

However, let's look at how we got here. The advent of the now ubiquitous smart phone is a key driver in the movement or integration of our lives with the online sphere. In 2007, Apple launched the iPhone and we have not looked back in our societal movement towards intertwining our lives and online technology. Our smart phones and tablets, and perhaps even smart watches smart speakers, smart TVs and in fact smart everything has changed how we shop, how we are entertained, how we manage money, how we get news, how we communicate and fundamentally how we order and make sense of our lives. We are increasingly embracing new technologies, and these often have huge benefits. Fundamentally, we changed how we live and we have done that for a reason. Wearable technology and smart scales have provided data suggestions and comparisons around our health and in turn led to bespoke and targeted suggestions, which previously was the domain of individual personal trainers. We communicate globally, video chat instant communication and social media allows us to maintain and benefit from international peer groups. A revolution in financial data and apps have reinvigorated pension savings in younger generations, have brought people's finances together in one place and given people control over them. In terms of knowledge consumption and generation, online courses from American Ivy League universities are freely available to learn from. Using online platforms, people can learn key skills for data coding for programming from industry experts. Already people can gain specific training directly from the companies they want to work for. Again though, the societal issues around this, and the inequality issues around this, and not inconsiderable, a continually online jobseeker can benefit from relevant training courses from the top universities in the world, the jobseeker using their local library on an ad hoc, once or twice a week basis to search for and apply for this, will simply not be able to take advantage of these options. Let us consider two equal jobseekers, both with equal skill sets both who come across their 'dream job' advert, working in project management. Of course, it doesn't have to be project management, but it can conceivably be any occupation; however, one of these job seekers is constantly online they have 24/7 access to the Internet; the other jobseeker equal in skill set has only ad hoc access to the online world. The first jobseeker firstly has the opportunity to further scope out the job on LinkedIn, they have the ability to look at other people in the organisation doing the same role and look at their skill sets, their training, their attributes. Then after working out any skills deficit, they have the option via a free Massive Open Online Course (MOOC), YouTube video or other online course, the ability to fill that skills deficit. For example, a quick search of Coursera, a popular online learning site, provides several free courses in project management with particular specialisms in construction project management, engineering project management and so on. The point here is that the continually online jobseeker has a distinct advantage over the ad hoc online jobseeker. In order to create a level unfair playing field, to facilitate worker benefits from the ABC economy, universal high-speed continual Internet access must be provided, but of course with a very strong consideration of the wellbeing aspect of this.

We have seen how technology is now so intertwined with our lives, in a way that was simply unimaginable before the millennium, even the dot-com boom companies and our burgeoning relationship with the online world in the early 2000s is as nought compared to our relationship with technology today. A simple mobile phone, a simple hand-held device, is in fact anything but simple. Most people's smart phones maintain their continual online presence, worker well-being is being threatened by the prevalence of email or mobile and the idea that one should always be contactable. It is to many companies' credit that employee well-being and email rules around contact hours and off time are being developed. It is notable however that in many cases pressure to be always available comes directly from the worker due to societal, rather than organisational pressures, to be permanently online and available. Too often though an organisational policy falls in place of a line managers or division head's example of out of hours working. A smart phone connects individuals to their email accounts to their social media apps to their banks and investments, to their entertainments by podcast apps and online TV, often to the grocery shops their high-street stores, and even their favourite coffee shop via the app. It is little wonder given the sheer power and flexibility of the smart phone that ideas of working, in the next mobile economy, revolve around constant online presence and smart phones.

THEMES OF WORK

Back to the framework, then. On first glance, the physical type looks a little out of place and in some ways protected from refinement, by the virtue of already being broken down by automation and the remaining processes, generally being geographically constrained. However, one imagines two distinct processes taking place. One on the supply side and one on the demand side. On the supply side, the decrease in skill required to complete a process under the creative, technical or people-based themes will decrease the supply of workers for the physical theme. On the demand side, then the physical type work, one of the few remaining specialisms not transferrable across the above matrix could become more exclusive and sought after.

Ultimately, via numerous refinement cycles, the ABC economy will reduce work to a number of themes with specialisms crossing those themes, these specialisms will become skills with more transferability across the themes and towards a possible end of attributes or traits. As the specialisms become skills and the transferability across the themes increases, the volume of workers able to complete these processes will increase, but the real volume of processes needing completing will increase at a faster rate.

The above sections represent our view of the culmination of a number of (super)trends in the global economy and whilst there are numerous paths and directions of these trends. We believe that the core overarching theme of the breaking down of the work output into its fundamental processes will result in an economy with work based on thematic microtasks and processes.

Much of the later chapters are built from this notion of work developing into a series of unrelated (from the point of the individual worker) microtasks, supported by real-time infinitely divisible payments and immutable transparent information. As mentioned earlier, this is part of an ongoing supertrend in the global economy

A WORKER WILL HAVE A NUMBER OF SPECIALISMS

In the previous section, we presented a possible future grid or types of work themes, these were we suggested grouping tasks and processes into four broad categories. These we called Physical, Creative, Technical and People-Based. Whatever the themes will eventually be, in short, we postulate that work will be broken down into a small number of types of microtask, and that these will continue to be refined in the ABC economy.

So then, what will a worker do? A specialism in one particular microtask is unlikely to provide a worker with enough wellbeing, fulfilment, interest and not forgetting remuneration to see to their needs. The traditional view of an occupation is failing in this microtask economy, and even having a number of specialisms within a particular field is unlikely to provide long-term stability and satisfaction. Earlier we argue that the specialisms and skills in a particular theme will ultimately be refined to only cross theme specialisms, especially around the notions of subjectivity, care and physical work. Likewise, as many tasks become further refined, the nanotask or picotask perhaps, the requisite skill set diminishes to the eventual notion that *any task can be completed to the same standard by anyone*. Traditionally, tasks with a high supply of labour have often been associated with low wages, poor conditions and precarity. In the next chapter, we will look at the specific conditions in the ABC economy which could prevent this universal labour potential from decreasing conditions and pay for all.

For now though, we will take the argument that most work will become a series of microtasks and as each output process is broken down further the microtask becomes more simple and the skill level required to complete the microtask to the appropriate standard decreases. The end conclusion of this process is that most microtasks have a near universal labour supply and that for the majority of microtasks completed online that labour supply is virtually instant and omnipresent.

How, then, will people market themselves for work? We can envisage a ratings system, not dissimilar to existing ratings and review systems for drivers, products and customer services, though with policy intervention to remove issues. We can see how even in today's process economy, a bad review can spell disaster for the individual.

PAYMENT, INCOME AND STABILITY?

We argue that the corporate coins will compete with and actively challenge sovereign currency and that it is a kind of semantic trap to compare cryptocurrency or cryptoassets with existing financial products.

> 'Government is given a false sense of familiarity
> by the currency part of the phrase. They think that
> this is something we have seen before, something
> we can control. The potential here is so much more
> than that.'[1]

However, it is useful when considering the behavioural and consumer responses to new corporate currencies to consider our response to our increasingly cashless world. Our increasing acceptance of cashlessness is a key facilitator of online corporate-cryptocurrencies.

The move towards a cashless economy continues apace. With a recent local example, being the option of contactless payments offered by bus companies in Greater Manchester. This trend is the continuation of a historical precedent beginning with the undersea telegraph linking New York and London, which electronically connected two global financial hubs. We will look at the rise of money replacements from the perspective of business and the consumer. It may come as no surprise that profit is a key motive in the rise of 'cashlessness' and the extra convenience of say contactless payment for the consumer is matched by greater profits for business and banking. However, is this really a case where everyone wins?

Banks and businesses, as a rule, dislike cash. They like what it represents, numbers in their accounts, but cash itself is difficult to store, a security risk, expensive to process and the main reason for costly bank branches having to be open. If we were to eliminate cash as a means of exchange and replace it with electronic transfer, then large amounts of costly infrastructure (generally the worker) is no longer required. In a world where 'contactless is king', cashing up, bank runs, change requirements and so on are no longer required. Nor are their associated staff. Physical banks are not required, ATMs reduced the need for bank branches, the cashless economy removes the need entirely. A huge corporation which doesn't trust its staff sees great advantage in not holding cash.

Let's return then to the profit motive. A cashless society generates convenience for the consumer, additional profit for business and banks. The convenience of a cashless economy is paid for by the removal of jobs associated with cash; of course this adds onto further innovation, stores where purchases are automatically debited no longer need check out staff, but self check-outs. We no longer need train conductors, but tap in systems. Consider self-check in hotels, self-check out in supermarkets, online shopping and so on, these are facilitated by doing away with the need for cash. Banks have an additional profit lever, a constraint on bank lending (and thus profit) is the requirement to provide individuals with accounts their money in cash if demanded. If we remove this demand, we remove a cheque on bank profit. Remember innovation towards cashlessness comes from profit-making firms, would a bank innovate with the aim of their reducing profitability?

A cashless economy benefits business and banks, what then do you pay for the convenience? Well, assuming that you don't have a job that will be lost through the move towards cashlessness, there is a big cost to you for the convenience of a cashless economy. You spend more of your money when it is easier for you to do so.

Let's consider the helpful tools which exist on most of your online shopping experiences. Why do you think most sites will store your card details? If at the end of your impulse shop you had to go and find your card, put in the numbers and details, billing address etc., you may re-evaluate the purchase. The site which stores your details gives you an easier route to spending. In order to cut impulse spending, delete your card details from being stored. Actually paying for something gives you a moment to consider the purchase – great for the buyer, bad for the seller. Would you spend as much if you had to post a cheque for payment?

As subscription services have long discovered, if you don't want people to do something, make it harder for them. Your monthly free trial in which you gave your card details upfront is likely to turn into a regular expense. Likewise, why do you think we pay for subscription services via card payment rather than direct debit? It is far easier to cancel a direct debt. A cancelled card is now more of an inconvenience than ever; previous we had only to learn a new PIN. Now your Netflix,

Amazon, Spotify and so on subscriptions need to be updated if you get a new card.

Think about why numerous banks are offering you the ability to 'freeze' your card, instead of reporting it lost or stolen. This is because individuals are becoming increasingly reluctant to report a card as lost, as quite simply the administrative costs to the user are really very high. A standard individual may now have their card details lodged with huge numbers of low-value subscriptions and applications, whereas previously most electronic payment was larger scale and based around standing orders and direct debits. Now, if you lose your bank card, you may have to update your Amazon account, Netflix account, public transport apps, coffee shop apps, grocery payment apps, the applications you use to buy your lunch at work, Ebay, Gumtree and Depop accounts and so on. Previously when getting a new phone the biggest inconvenience may have been transferring over your contacts list, now the numerous apps, which you use to navigate your day-to-day activities, may vanish, may not be updated or may all need logging into again.

Moving away from the online world, what do you think of as money? Ask a child to draw a picture of money and they will generally draw notes and coin, our piggy banks collected notes and coin. This association is strong; you feel less of a sense of loss paying with a cashless system rather than handing over a pound note. Nearly 20 years ago, marketing academics, Prelec and Simester demonstrated that people were prepared to pay up to twice as much for the same thing compared to cash buyers (in their case sports tickets).[2] Ask yourself if contactless payment systems have made it easier for you to spend your money. Is the spending you do now psychologically linked to what you perceive as money. Contactless payment via your phone is far removed from the process of using cash. What about when you use your new Corporate Cryptocurrency?

Close your eyes and picture some money, what do you see? It's probably a picture in some way of notes and coin (or even delving into our past, some gold!). It is unlikely you see your credit card or your phone, what then do you think you are spending when you tap your phone to buy your lunch?

EVOLVING MONEY?

The rise of cryptocurrency is an unprecedented and as yet unexplored challenge to the economic view of money and the monetary system. Elsewhere we contend that cryptocurrency is symptomatic of the decline of the state and suggest that the challenge to the *status quo* is so colossal that the economic language required to understand it is in development. Indeed, it is a reassurance to policy makers and power that the language of money is used, this presents a known challenge, a familiar disruption in the guise of new technology. The challenge of cryptocurrency is so much more, a new rise in individualism and non-state power with the potential to radically alter the systems in which we live.

The evolution of cryptocurrency is alien to our understanding of the evolution of process, we contest an evolution based on use and perception, with the next generation(s) of cryptocurrency moving further away from institutions which would seek to control them. We propose a teleological understanding and classification which places current cryptocurrencies into two generations, the akin to currency as we understand it and the second based on an evolution of this system. This second generation when considered from a behavioural viewpoint is so far removed from our understanding of currency that were it not for the comfort and familiarity of the currency portion of the term, policy and scholars would be classifying these in a whole new way. Indeed, we contest that part of the slow policy response to cryptocurrency is institutional misunderstanding of their use. They have evolved past the traditional confines and understandings of currency. Furthermore, this evolution is continuing apace, we later speculate on what the third generation may be, but this process is ongoing. This is evolution not at a historical pace, but at an online one where cryptocurrencies for new and as yet unforeseen purpose and activity can be developed in a matter of hours.

We use a behavioural and perception of use concept to create the generations of cryptocurrency framework. Of course, individual existing cryptocurrencies may cross the generational boundary. It is when the idea of use and understanding is used that we can begin to see that the evolution of cryptocurrency takes a unique form, moving away from standard notions of institutionalisation.

We posit a framework based on three levels of understanding and use, where movement in speed of understanding and capacity to understand suggests changing power dynamics. Ultimately throughout the development of cryptocurrency, the state or regulator's understanding diminishes. The three levels we use to determine generation are regulatory understanding, corporate understanding and individual understanding.

The first generation of cryptocurrency then has a familiar feel to it. Society understands the notion of money, of which the first generation of cryptocurrency seeks to emulate (and ultimately surpass). The state can regulate an idea of cryptocurrency which is simply money, the Central Bank and Tax Authority are versed in understanding proxies for domestic currency, gold, silver, foreign currency, vouchers and so on can all be assimilated into the existing structures. Likewise, corporations have a full understanding of this sphere, they seek to generate more profit in whatever their reporting currency is and as such are able to subsume a further store of value into their processes. Society too can fully understand a further proxy for their money – the vast majority of people have used alternative currencies at various points in their lives, be it book tokens, foreign currencies or even Disney Dollars!

The first generation of cryptocurrency, then, is a familiar one, just another proxy for money which will ultimately be converted from the individual into profit and tax receipts. For example, Bitcoin, arguably the first major and well-known cryptocurrency, does just this. It allows individuals to store their wealth and be rewarded for their labour, in a different proxy but one that serves the same purpose, firms can accept it for payment, it has a tangible domestic currency convertible value and as such can be incorporated into the state via the tax system. We can regulate it in terms of transparency and consumer protection, but this is an age old, accessible and understandable process.

It is the movement from first to second generation which challenges notions of institutionalism, regulation and power.

We can see how the next evolution of cryptocurrency goes beyond the understanding of the state and the capture of corporations outside of the target of the 'crypto'. The level of analysis and unit of understanding is the individual. Second generation cryptocurrencies are removed from the notion of money in the existing economic system. They may diminish in use or value if collected in volume, they may generate activity which has no monetary (as measured in traditional terms) value but forms part of new business models and they may provide for a need, want or purpose outside of our current economic thinking. Ultimately, the individual can understand and 'value' this want, even when it is outside of a monetary calculation, Business may account for this activity in terms of brand loyalty or market share, the state is outside this calculation as they are outside of taxing 'intangibles'.

**Case Study – The History of Financial Innovation:
Where Are We and How Did We Get Here?**

In order to understand how the future pay system in the
Bitwork world may work, it is useful to recap briefly a
considerable portion of our payments of financial history. What we will be able to see through this recap
is a progression towards a much more flexible idea
of what money is and how we receive and spend it.
It is useful to consider the behavioural aspects of our
relationship with money and to look at this evolution
through the ages. We wear relevant, invite the reader to
consider their own relationship with their money as we
go through this section.

There's always been relationship between data
and money. In the past, the first technology or system
around money concerns systems and records for taxes,
for debt, for construction, and even for welfare. Systems
of records existed in parishes to facilitate the new and
old pause, the recording of family land rights titles and
privileges has all been associated with money. Skipping
through ideas of barter economies to what is known
as commodity money. Commodity money is what we
traditionally think of as money, our idea of money that
comes from films and stories, from fairytales, the idea
of money as gold or silver precious metal or gemstone,
something that is traded because of its intrinsic value,
and something that gleans value for its rarity. The interesting question of course, is how we get from the idea
of gold and something very tangible as money, from a
gold coin ops to the idea that something as ephemeral
as a contactless payment is money. In order to understand this, we need to travel back around a 150 years,

when the first transatlantic telegraph cable was laid connecting major financial centres of New York and London. This system went on to connect the European financial centres and later the global financial centres and crucially for the first time we start seeing the idea of finance as data. The evolution of this system is our current system, and in fact more undersea cable is being lead than ever before and this is the cope with the increased flow of data. You may have heard the expression data are the new oil. Your data, the digital form of your everyday activities, are becoming increasingly valuable. The laying of the transatlantic telegraph marked the first point in our recent financial history were the foundations, and the cornerstones of our existing system. With revolutionary improvements and inventions, this system continued and the next major innovations came around World War II, these innovations concerned cryptography and code breaking and, in particular, led to the inventions of computer technology and algorithmic thinking, which eventually have led to AI and machine learning of the current ground breaking revolutions in technology that we are currently witnessing.

Skipping forward a century or so after the first transatlantic telegraph, Barclays launched the first automatic teller machine (ATM). This event is seismic in our understanding and shaping of societies relationship with money. Gone is the idea of the necessity of human-to-human interaction in the money system; gone is the idea of meticulous planning around your own personal money supply, and gone is some of the mystique of the bank. Money, albeit still in the form of paper money, start to become readily available. The very first credit card was introduced in 1946, however, it is really in 1967 where we start to see the beginnings of digitisation, conversion of analogue systems, hand-written ledgers from a bank clerk, to something that is machine readable. Individuals began to have relation-ships with money that didn't require human interven-tion, or at least visible human intervention. This really use the popular creation or idea money is electronic data. Personal finance innovations begin to come thick and fast, in 1971, the first electronic stock exchange was launched, the NASDAQ. Soon after very few none-lectronic exchange is survived, and from this we get the idea of digital money and an automated process, so much so that today is rare for human to be actu-ally trading directly, and instead algorithms automated trades are the norm.

As soon as we moved to the idea of money as a data or electronic entity, we free markets to expand. For example, in today's global foreign exchange markets, over \$6 trillion is traded on a daily basis, and virtually none of this is in cash. In the 1980s, the ATM network becomes interconnected, and individuals can access money from any account via any ATM, anywhere the 1980s and 1990s began our journey into online bank-ing, which increased in the 2000s and exploded with the advent of smart phones and devices.

In early 2000s, we had a situation, or system, or elec-tronic money being the norm, with financial technology (early FinTech) providing platforms and the acceptance that money is an abstract digital concept, rather than notes and coin. An idea that geographic boundaries are not a barrier to money and that we are increasingly accepting of the inter-twining of money and technology. In 2007, Vodafone launched M-Pesa, this was the mobile phone-based payment system which quite simply brought significant amounts of the population of Kenya into financial services, and these are both revolutionary and are great examples of the benefits that this sort of innovation can bring.

Then, the 2008 global financial crisis happened. This damaging worldwide crisis in finance had devastating short-term effects on individuals, we talk of lost generations. In the UK, we still talk of returning back to pre-2008 levels of income and stability. One of the most pernicious and long-term effects of the 2008 global financial crisis is simply a continued, societal loss of trust in 'the system'. By the system, we mean the fundamental and foundational institutions of our economy, this loss of trust transmitted from the banks, to the regulators, and to the government as a whole. It is not surprising, but key to our analysis, the 2008 marked a significant turning point in public opinion away from trust in traditional financial and governance institutions to the large technology firms. It is this lack of trust and increase in regulation, to attempt to prevent the next crisis, which has in essence caused a seismic shift both in, our societal relationships and understanding of finance, and the institutions which facilitate our financial lives. The 2008 global financial crisis led to:

1) Diminishing trust in traditional institutions.

2) A credit crunch.

3) Significant job losses being the financial industry.

The lack of trust in traditional institutions, allowed for a shift in trust to the familiar and burgeoning big tech brands. The so-called credit crunch, in essence a fear and regulatory driven reduction in credit availability, even to individuals with good credit histories, provided excess demand for finance which was not being met. Finally, significant job losses in the financial industry, as is usually the case, tended to disproportionately hit newer, younger, more technologically skilled recent recruits. These three consequences of the 2008 global financial crisis quite simply created the demand and talent for alternative finance.

Haddad et al. (2019) state that:

> *The supply of fintech startups, in contrast, consists of the entrepreneurs who are ready to undertake self-employment (Choi and Phan, 2006). Such a supply might be driven by a large number of investment bankers who lost their jobs after the financial crises and are now eager to use their finance skills in a related and promising financial sector.*

For instance Revolut's CEO said:[3]

> *Many of Lehman Brothers' top employees who left in the aftermath of its collapse decided to start their own businesses. A generation of entrepreneurs rose from the ashes, but many were disillusioned with the financial system. At the time, I was working as a derivatives trader at Lehman's when Nomura bought our division, but I ended up taking an offer from Credit Suisse, where I eventually met Vlad Yatsenko, Revolut's co-founder and*

CTO. We were both frustrated with the fees charged to send money abroad and launched Revolut in July 2015 as a way to rebuild the industry from the ground up using technology

2008 is when it all changed. Lack of trust in the system combined with new talent and demand, rapidly saw numerous financial innovations (what we generally understand that the beginnings of FinTech). 2008 saw the release of the Bitcoin White Paper (including its foundational blockchain technology), 2009 saw Bitcoin theory turn into reality and marked the beginning of several thousand alternative cryptocurrencies. 2010 saw the release of contactless and the beginnings of mobile phone payments, which fundamentally changes our relationship with money. 2015 introduces us to wearable devices and the idea that our watch, etc. can perform the same functions as banks. Our behaviour is significantly begin to change at this time, Bill sharing apps begin to become commonplace, intertwining behavioural and psychological theory combine with technology to provide solutions to hitherto untreated social stigma's such as simply asking your friends for money they may owe you. The introduction of biometric locks on mobile phones, provide (at least the illusion of) security meaning more people are more likely to use their apps for financial transactions. Companies begin to launch specific loyalty-based apps which facilitate payments by QR codes, giving the company huge power and insight over your data. Data, as previously mentioned, are fast becoming money or at least a proxy for money. 2020 may see the launch of Libra, Facebook's cryptocurrency, which has every possibility of becoming electronic money in every conceivable sense. All these developments, and the future was to come, are fundamentally changing our relationship with money. Money may no longer be the preserve of governments, something that weep you of as notes or coins or even tangible, most of us already only relate to money as numbers on a screen and as the techniques of machine learning of big data analysis are further applied to our personal data, this process will continue at an exponential rate. Facebook's potential entry into the financial world, marks the West's shift from FinTech to TechFin, facilitated not only by technological developments, but regulatory and governance ones as well. For instance, the new EU banking directive provides access to banking data by start-ups, traditional banking institutions are slow and cumbersome in this new world, access to their data further facilitates the shift from FinTech to TechFin.

Libra is TechFin and a key example of how the big technology firms are rebuilding financial structures.

Here, we would invite the reader to consider their own cash usage. The vast majority of one's wage is never seen in cash, for a standard individual, where you can mortgage or rent takes up a sizeable portion of their income, this disappears from the accounts generally in an electronic payment usually direct debit or standing order, most if not all of your bills are paid electronically. Your utilities bill, mobile phone contract, car insurance, car payment, etc. will usually all be direct debits. Of course, this being said, it is most unlikely that prior its deposit into your bank account,

you see your wage in cash. Virtually every organisation which pays its employees does so via bank transfer and does so electronically. For instance, when you
are doing your day-to-day spending, generally public
transport, certainly in cities, has some form of electronic payments default, whether this is contactless tapping
out, payment via an app or online purchase of a smart-
card. Your supermarket shop, particularly if shopping
online, is likely to be a credit or debit card payment as
is virtually every other transaction you make. It is far
more likely, that you have recently seen a sign saying
'we are a cashless organisation, we only accept credit
or debit cards', than a sign saying 'cash only'. Unless
you have a specific reason to use cash, with common
reasons including taxi cabs (though again these are
increasingly becoming cashless), purchases in cash only
environments, such as markets and fairs (which again
are increasingly becoming cashless) or level payments
for services (which again are increasingly becoming
cashless, with HMRC support). It is increasingly likely
that in the last month you did not deposit cash in or
withdraw cash from your bank account, and instead
received and made all payments electronically. It is
interesting to see the proliferation of apps designed for
parents to use to provide a child with electronic pocket
money. Our societal and traditional relationship with
cash has already disappeared; banks are increasingly
issuing debit cards without raised numerals for them to
better fit into phone cases. The term wallet has a new
meaning, which is an electronic repository for electronic money. The soon to be commonplace example is
Calibra, Facebook's electronic wallet which will hold

its electronic money, Libra. Ask yourself how your relationship and understanding of money has changed over the last decade – do you spend differently; do you act differently? Has the contactless £30 limit changed your spending behaviours? Now consider how you are spending behaviours may change with future developments further altering our idea of money.

BEFORE THERE WAS DECENTRALISED MONEY, THERE WAS DECENTRALISED BANKING .... A REVIEW OF THE FRINGE LITERATURE

It is worth noting here that arguments around the decentralisation of money have in various economic fields and guises been around for a very long time and stretch into the macro-working of the economy. Many libertarian fields in heterodox economics consider that state intervention in the money supply is fundamentally responsible for economic crisis, and whilst neither of the authors wholly subscribe to these views, it is worth detailing them below, even to get a feel for this ultimate deregulation in the economy and what type of economy may arise from the removal of the state from the monetary supply.

Rothbard (2001) states that 'the economist who sees the free market working splendidly in all other fields should hesitate for a long time before dismissing it in the sphere of money', in the current climate of a clamour for further government involvement in the financial sector[4]; it is understandable that this concept is dismissed outright and its theoretical basis forgotten. Yet, cryptocurrencies may be the next stage of the market infiltrating the monetary process. We argue that they represent the ultimate 'denationalisation of money', making corporations and individuals the powerbrokers in the new monetary sphere, and a consideration of the effects is useful to understanding both the end effect of decentralisation of money as one of the underlying philosophies behind cryptocurrencies.

WHY CRITICS OF THE STATE IN THE MONETARY SYSTEM CONSIDER IT TO BE PROBLEMATIC?

The current monetary system which allows, via some form of government intervention, the creation of credit, as the banking system is not subject to traditional legal principles (de Soto, 2006). However, the literature suggests that it is precisely this privilege of the banking system to create money seemingly from thin air (de Soto, 2010) that is flawed. The literature considers the creation in this way to be theoretically unsound (Hayek, 2007; de Soto, 2010). This is as, considering theories of capital and Hayekian Business Cycles, the viewpoint of the literature is that the credit creation prowess of fractional reserve banking (FRB) leads to severe malinvestment in the boom which eventually and inevitably causes its collapse (Hayek, 2007). This concept is derived from the work of Mises (1980) and Hayek and in a very simple form states that investment ultimately built on savings is far more stable and long term than investment built on credit. The limitations of the existing system therefore lie in the examination of a boom created in a fractional reserve environment. It is a frequent feature of the literature to discuss the popularity of such credit expansions in the short run, both with politicians and the general public (Hayek, 2007, de Soto, 2010). de Soto (2010) states how in a credit expansion, entrepreneurs are usually pleased as they can obtain cheap finance for virtually any project. As savings are not required to fund the investment, there is no reduction in the

demand at final consumption, commodity prices tend to rise
and thus their representation on stock markets, at this stage
of the boom it appears that an individual's wealth can be
raised through no prior sacrifice of consumption (de Soto,
2006, 2010). Politicians are usually myopic enough to enjoy
being associated with the boom and the perceived increase
in national wealth, and as a bonus see government revenues
increase year on year (de Soto, 2010). Booms based on credit
expansion appear to make irrelevant the law of scarcity and
encourage investment outside the real abilities of the economy (Muller, 2001). The literature emphasises the discord
in the market between the individuals who have no wish to
increase savings and investors who are relying on the credit
creation of banks, and describes how the market when unim-
peded by government, is a dynamically efficient mechanism
which will move to correct this process. A consideration of
this correction process further highlights the limitations of
the existing FRB system; the material considers there to be
six microeconomic reactions by the market which will occur
to correct the bank credit expansion.[5] To summarise, firstly,
there will be a price raise in labour, natural resources and
commodities as saving has not increased reducing resource
use at the final stage of consumption and with resources
utilised at this stage, production at stages further from
competition will compete for more limited labour and
resources using the credit gained from the FRB system. Secondly, the price of consumer goods will rise more quickly
than the rise of the price of labour, natural resources and
commodities. This occurs when there is an excess of money at
the final stage of consumption at the same time as a reduction
in the supply of consumption goods as focus shifts to more
distant consumption. This allows for the third effect of a rise
in calculable accounting profits of firms in closest proximity
to end stage consumption and a stagnation of capital good

industries whose costs increase at a greater level than their turnover. Fourthly and crucially, the Ricardo effect occurs, with end stage consumption enjoying increasing prices, real wages begin to decrease and firms begin to substitute now relatively cheaper labour for capital, further depressing the capital producing firms.[6] The observed effect is an increase in the loan rate of interest as the credit expansion slows, something that always occurs, due to the increased purchasing power of funds (de Soto, 2010). Hayek (1937) notes how people seeking finance at this stage begin a 'fight to the death' for additional finance, further increasing the price of the loan. The cumulative effect of these discussed events is simply that firms operating in those stages furthest from consumption realise that they are making severe accounting losses. de Soto states that these losses when compared with profits at consumption reveal the error of financing investment with credit and there is now a pressing need for ceasing and liquidating the flawed investment projects. These microreactions emphasise the limitations of the existing FRB system, a financial crisis, perhaps in this light better termed a financial correction by the market, looms the instant it is realised by the market that the actual worth of the bank credit created is far less than was supposed. In essence, the real liabilities (deposits) of the banks are greater than the created assets (loans) and as such the banks are in significant danger of collapse. The literature explains how this financial crisis is *not* the cause of the recession (correction for the Hayek), but a sign that it has already started.

The Hayekian view that government legislative privilege and central bank support allowing for bank credit creation, ensures that financial crisis and thus recession are inevitable (de Soto, 2010). de Soto (2010) argues that the expansionary cycle that precipitated the 2008 crisis began in misguided efforts to stimulate the American economy from its turmoil in 2001, where state intervention through the central bank began a significant upswing in credit expansion completely unsupported by any increase in saving.[7,8] The argument is continued with an analysis of the speculative bubble in property and commodity prices caused, according to de Soto by the inflation of fiduciary media usually offered to the market at an exceptionally low (or even negative in real terms) rates. Hayekian theories of the unsustainability of an artificial credit expansion and an inflation of fiduciary media provide a context for the discussion, with de Soto (2010) stating that the specific factors causing the end of the monetary boom were a rise in commodity prices (particularly oil), the sub-prime mortgage miscalculation and the failure of important banking organisations occurring where the market realised the economic miscalculations they had made. It is emphasised again that due to the fundamental limitations of the current system that the crisis and recession are inevitable consequences of the systems reliance on FRB and unsustainable credit expansion. de Soto (2009) argues that the triggers of the monetary crisis are dependent on the circumstances surrounding it, but the crisis itself will always occur as a result of the systemic flaw of the existing system. Miller (2009) argues that Hayekian analysis of trade cycles has relevance for the recent financial crisis stating that future economic historians may assess the recent recession as less deep than the Great Depression, but more Hayekian.

The reforms discussed are systemic reforms aimed at a complete alteration of the existing system and not simply reforms to the current system; proposals discussed are not minor technicalities of finance (Hayek, 2007). In the first instance, when considering the literature concerning the structural reform, given the acceptance of the unsustainability of FRB (Hayek, 2007), the theoretical basis for an investment system based on savings is a frequent feature. The argument is a chronological progression of ideas discussed in the literature. The step by step progression is collected in the work of de Soto (2006).

de Soto collects the pieces of the Hayekian puzzle and demonstrates that they work together in explaining economic phenomena (Van den Hauwe, 2006). Broadly speaking, the argument for saving-based investment is based on Hayek's theories of capital and is contrary to the mainstream paradox of thrift (Hayek, 1975). We suggest that it is helpful for understanding to consider the temporal nature of the productive process, where in the market most productive factors produce goods not intended to mature immediately and are expected to be demanded at a more distant stage. de Soto (2009) suggests a dramatic increase in savings to demonstrate the theory, the savings rate increases and therefore the subjective time preference of economic agents must decrease. This forces three microeconomic effects in the market. Firstly, the profitability of firms closest to consumption will decrease as demand decreases due to the increase in savings. Profitability of firms further from consumption will remain unchanged and thus economic activity within these firms will be more attractive to entrepreneurs and investors, firms will therefore be encouraged to wherever possible, transfer their activities from those near consumption to those further away. Secondly, an increase in savings will drive down the interest rate and thus reduce the discounting effect of interest on future profits, it becomes even clearer that profitability further from consumption in capital goods industries is greater than that in consumer goods for immediate consumption.[9] The increase in the savings rate has firstly reduced demand at consumption, thus reducing profitability at this end stage and secondly decreased the interest rate, allowing the legitimate calculation of greater profits away from consumption in capital good industries. Thirdly, the market experiences what Hayek terms the Ricardo effect, where assuming that incomes remain constant, an increase in savings will lead to a decrease in demand at consumption, hence a decrease in price of consumer goods, therefore increasing the purchasing power of income *ceteris paribus*. With real wages increased, firms will now substitute the relatively less expensive capital goods for labour, in the unhampered market labour displaced by cheaper capital goods is demanded in their production (de Soto, 2009). The literature suggests that the culmination of these three effects is a longer productive process less focussed on final consumption, this process being sustainable as it is backed by previous saving (de Soto, 2006).

PRE-CRYPTOCURRENCIES REFORM

The literature for monetary reform based around these ideas of capital theory and sustainable money tends to differ in two areas. Firstly, the identity of the money producer is in dispute, some are happy with money being produced by governments (White, 1989), whereas others, for instance, Hayek (2007) argue that market produced money is more appropriate for the market economy.[10] Mises (1966) would further reduce any state role by only allowing it to perform a conversion function, that is the state would operate a mint converting privately produced pure metal into coin and allow for the conversion of perfectly redeemable money substitutes into this coin, Rothbard (2001) has the only reform of complete private production with the ideal of a pure gold standard. However, due to the financial crisis, such ideas are becoming less of a 'fringe' argument and meriting contemporary discussion. For instance, Hulsman (2008) discusses Mises' gold standard arguments, W.R. White (2008) the head of the Monetary and Economic Department at the Bank for International Settlements has called for a return to a more rule-based system by reinstating gold as the reserve currency. de Soto (2010) argues that in response to the recent crisis, what is required is the privatisation of fiduciary media then its replacement with a 'classic pure gold standard'. The fallout from the East Asian Financial Crisis in the late 1990s prompted Reisman (2000) to state that 'the goal of monetary reform should be a 100% gold standard'. From a consideration of the literature, it becomes clear that an explanation for the absence of more discussion on the issue, is the transition difficulty of readopting such a standard which is almost universally accepted as being close to insurmountable, with Van den Hauwe (2006) describing the economics of transition to a full gold standard worthy of legitimate research in themselves.[11]

The second differentiation in the literature concerns the design of money substitutes, Selgin (1988) states how the issue of fiduciary media is a right of freedom of contract. Mises (1980) has the view that there is no legal right for the issuing of any fiduciary media and only for the issuing of perfectly redeemable money substitutes; this can be seen in the contrast between Sennholz (1985, 1987) and Mises. Sennholz envisaged a natural limit faced by banks when issuing fiduciary media due to reserve and withdrawal requirements, Mises takes the view that there are no such limits and the banks would be able to inflate fiduciary media without restriction.[12]

Hayek's views on private property are contrary to those of Mises, Rothbard differs from both in his view point and this is evident in a consideration of these authors' proposals in the literature.[13]

Rothbard's (2001) proposal involves the dissolution of the Federal Reserve (FED). In the case of the FED, its assets will be cashed in to repay its liabilities and its regulatory functions absolved, all state issued assets held by the FED will be cancelled and the gold held will be revalued to allow for 100% redemption of FED-issued fiat money. This gold would then be claimed by the fiat holders, banks would therefore have their reserves fully transformed into gold and thus they would be able to provide their own fully backed private money substitute without any state privilege. Mises' (1980) proposal for reform is by contrast less far reaching (Herbener, 2002), but in line with the literature surveyed, seeks for the prevention of unsustainable monetary and credit expansion. Mises would freeze the volume of FED notes and prevent the issuing of subsequent fiduciary media, concurrently the gold market would be freed of any state interference, once a natural price of gold had been achieved by the market (Mises allows for a transition period), it is proposed that a conversion agency is created by the state to enable holders of FED notes to convert to gold at parity value, to allow for the usage of gold coin in the monetary process and to prevent state inflation of the monetary supply, Mises proposed the withdrawal of medium sized dollar bills to be replaced directly with gold coin. The state conversion agency could only issue more notes if its gold store increased or as a direct replacement for old or damaged notes. Mises' proposes reform prevents further inflation by preventing the future issue of fiduciary media whilst preventing damage caused to the economy by sudden deflation of the monetary supply. These reforms do not go as far as Rothbard, maintaining the level of money in the system does not perform the liquidation of mal-investment described earlier, also the inclusion of the state and the continued existence of the central bank as well as the state conversion agency allow for possible state interference.[14,15] The proposed reforms of Hayek would abolish any restriction in the production of money and end any legal tender laws, a process which would end the state monopoly in the production of money. This, according to Hayek (2007), would motivate the private banks to produce their own money, which would have to be stable to provide the users with an acceptable means of exchange, with the users now having a choice in their money use, if any money is not stable and thereby not an adequate means of exchange the market will reject it. When the market accepts a money as secure and stable, this money will take precedent over state produced money if the state produced money does not equal the level of security and stability of the privately produced source. Hayek highlights that the main problem of his proposal would be in convincing the public of the suitability of money produced by private enterprise, this of course translates directly into today where public opinion is particularly anti-bank. Sennholz's (1985) proposed reform, similarly to Hayek, would end any state monopoly of money production and provide the legal means for private money production and again, similar to Hayek, recognises that a major problem in this reform would be altering public perception of privately produced money. Sennholz (1985) firmly believes that good money will drive out bad, and that the state could only keep its position as primary money producer in the absence of an enforced monopoly privilege by providing money that is secure and stable and thus accepted by the market, with market free to choose, Sennholz argues that gold will become the most popular means of exchange. de Soto's (2006, 2010) proposed reforms are of particular interest to the consideration of cryptocurrencies as they develop the discussed reforms in a contemporary context and in the light of the current financial crisis. These reforms are based on the principle of a healthy process of capital accumulation through true savings and seek the complete eradication of the state from the monetary process, de Soto singularly in the literature places the blame for the recent financial turmoil and thus recession solely on the state in general and central banks in particular (de Soto 2010).

For Hayek, the end goal of monetary reform, that is to return to the highest stage of money market development as explained by Mises and Menger (explained in Herbener, 2002) with the market dominant in the monetary process and a secure and stable currency. The literature displays a variety of proposals for monetary reform. The end is the same, but the means can vary, dependant on the authors' adherence to branches of thought, for instance, Sennholz and Hayek see a competitive role with the state in money production, Mises envisages a state role in monetary conversion and Rothbard seeks for the total removal of the state from the entirety of the money process (Gertchev, 2004). The authors' views on deflation of the monetary supply against fixing its current level, the rights and functions of private property law and the nature or existence of a money substitute differentiate the literature.[16]

The primary aim of the 'denationalisation of money' requires the elimination or reduction of the role of the state in the monetary process, some thought is given to the likely efforts of the state to restore its involvement and associated benefits, it is acknowledged that the long-term success of any reform is dependent on preventing this (Herbener, 2002; Hulsman, 2008; de Soto, 2006). A criticism levied within the school against the majority of the reform proposals surveyed is the scope they provide for this to occur; Hayek notes that any crisis can be used by the state to justify increasing the money supply, Rothbard proposes the most complete permanent elimination of the state. The work of de Soto (2006, 2010), developed in the light of the recent financial crisis and recession, provide a contemporary relevance on this issue, de Soto (2006) considers that new cycles of artificial credit expansion and thus recession will inevitably occur unless the existing financial system is fundamentally redesigned to prevent artificial credit expansion. Mises' theory of the economic impossibility of socialism is applicable to government intervention in capitalist banking, the theory sets out how the state does not have the required information to succeed over the market, using this, de Soto (2006) argues that the state via central banks indulges in Hayek's fatal conceit in believing itself able to deliver the appropriate monetary policy in a dynamic circumstance for the benefit of the economy, and that central banks are directly responsible for the recent crisis. de Soto's (2006, 2010) proposed monetary reform includes the complete removal of central banks, this will provide two functions in restoring the monetary primacy of the market, it will remove state interference and ensure that a 100% reserve requirement on demand deposits is maintained through the removal of the lender of last resort from the monetary process.[17] Austrian theory is far from orthodox and not shared by many economists in practice or academia.

CAN CRYPTOCURRENCIES FIX THE SYSTEM?

It is clear that Hayek in the Denationalisation of Money did not envisage the technological advancement and societal and economic shifts which led to 'ordinary' individuals being able to create global monetary substitutes (e.g. Bitcoin). Hayek argued that the solution to the boom bust economic cycles caused by malinvestment, FRB and unconstrained credit lay in the removal of the state and its largesse from the monetary process. Previously, this has been imagined by the academy and society as per the previous section, it was not envisaged that globally accepted perfectly transparent individually created money substitutes would compete with national money and via this competition provide Hayek's stabilisation mechanism.

Denationalising the money supply for Hayek involved Banks making their own decisions regarding lending, making these transparent and relying on the market via consumers moving their deposits to coordinate sensible lending decisions. This is as without state involvement allowing for the expansion of the money supply, consumers would regulate the banks as their individual deposits are those being directly lent.

A currency coded on the blockchain is perfectly transparent, its functions are publicly available, if one owns a Bitcoin, they own a fixed portion of the total supply. The final amount of Bitcoin to exist is immutable, the pound in your bank account is a fluid proportion of the total money supply. So if a nation abandoned its currency and converted to Bitcoin, then its monetary expansion is determined not by political whim and action, but by a predefined code. This is not the space to address the ongoing battles and debates in economics surrounding the causes of crisis, but it is useful to note that proponents of cryptocurrency may have a wider economic ideology as well as individual level support form a decentralised currency, and it is useful to consider what an economy with a denationalised currency may look like.

WHAT WILL PEOPLE DO WITH THEIR MONEY?

A key consideration for financial crisis causation is moral hazard. A moral hazard is simply when an insurance against a particular risk makes that risk more likely to be taken, this is twofold within the financial system, firstly the deposit protection insurance aspect of individual savings, the ultimate guarantee of individual savers getting their money back in event of crisis helps support a too risky system as people are still prepared to deposit in it. This is of crucial importance, depositors and their willingness to deposit should provide an ultimate check on the financial system, one above the power and willingness of a regulator. In essence if depositors consider the financial system as a whole or any individual institution too risky, they will find alternative homes for their deposits. Quite simply this would mean that a financial system could not operate at a level of return above the market or natural rate of interest with a simple supply of deposit policy determining how much risk an institution could take. However, the insurance aspect means that depositors are happy to accept excess reward (a higher sector level of risk) as they face no individual risk (up to £85k). A custodian bank option has been suggested as a solution, that is, with a true risk-free deposit option the market could if they chose save securely and therefore there would be no need to insure against loss, for instance, if a saver chose to not keep their money in a custodian bank account then they could be assumed to accept the risk reward level of the financial system. As depositors are naturally risk averse, then in order to acquire their deposits the financial system would need to operate at a level of risk acceptable to the market. Unfortunately, this fails to take into account the confidence of an economy which may increase above these levels. We wonder if stablecoin cryptocurrencies could provide a type of custodian bank and if so, then what the policy and societal implications are for an economy where workers can personally and efficiently hedge their wealth if they lose confidence in their domestic currency.

MAINSTREAM MULTIPLE ROLE WORK

This is the idea, that in the ABC future, the majority of people, the norm will be multiple role work. However not in the way that we understand it today. Today, the common perception of multiple role work, is a collection of part-time, or temporary contracts in a small number of low skilled, potentially precarious, positions. The key commonality in these positions, generally being that they are low skilled and can de facto be done by anyone, with the defining feature that for the employee the particular role does not constitute enough activity to be appropriate of full-time working patterns. This means that in order to generate a full-time equivalent income the worker needs to be several of these ad hoc roles. The power dynamics here tend to rely solely with the organisation or hirer, this is not to say that in some cases the worker doing these roles does not benefit from some form of flexibility but for instance, they will not be able to negotiate improved terms for themselves.

Instead, we suggest a future where most workers in society will complete the microtasks which cannot be done by automation, as part of the algorithmised new economic output system. We class this as multiple role work, but potentially a better definition is of a highly multi-process role, the key defining feature of which is virtually every microtask completed, is completed for different organisations and algorithms. A further aspect of this, is that through machine learning and data generation from successful completion of the microtask the next iteration, request microtasks to be completed, will look different as AI continues to develop and continues to further breakdown its required inputs. It is not unreasonable to consider that even though, as discussed, we expect numerous microtasks from many different organisations the worker completing microtask platform, facilitated by smart contracts, may not even know who they are working for. In this future, your LinkedIn profile (or similar) could be your biggest asset, and ideas of platform working may come to the fore.

We need to query then, if this is just widespread self-employment scenario. If in fact the movement towards microtask completion, is not simply a continuation of the post-2008 trend towards more self-employment, more entrepreneurship, more start-ups. Can we simply conceptualise this as something with which we are all familiar? For example, a plumber may complete daily tasks for numerous different organisations. They may not even know exactly who they are working for, who owns the pipes they are fixing in an office block, is it the tenants, the management firm, the holding company or so on. They bill by invoice and receive payments on a regular basis. The technology developing the ABC is an improvement in efficiency in this area, instead of payment issues and bad debts arising from non-payment of invoice, we have smart contracts providing full security and cryptocurrencies facilitating real-time accurate payment. We could be tempted to argue, that microtask completion in the ABC, is nothing more than the evolution of self-employment, and the culmination of an ongoing trend away from employment. We suggest that in fact, this new world of work goes much further than this and the mainstream multiple role work in the ABC economy is a new way of coordinating and generating economic output and activity. We explore this further in the next chapter.

However, now let us briefly think of microtask completion in the ABC economy, as of this revolution of self-employment and the end stage of the growth of self-employment start-ups since 2008, what would this mean for society for all self-employed?

Self-employment provide numerous benefits to the individual, benefits around freedom, flexibility, choice and so on. It also comes with numerous costs, such as a lack of employment benefits and a lack of security. It is worth considering that in the blockchain-enabled world of smart contracts, much of these costs can be mitigated. In theory, the ABC world could generate workers with the freedom and flexibility of self-employment and the protections and benefits of employment. Is this not just though a pipedream, a perfect future that will never happen? It is reasonable to assume, that in a world of mass self-employment, each input–output-related smart contracts could integrate relatively seamlessly with the tax system to generate a highly efficient, actually real-time, Pay As You Earn (PAYE) system. If this is possible then several recent innovations in nudging worker behaviour could also be implemented. For example, we could have self-employed auto enrolment of pensions, we could have automatic national insurance contributions, automatic saving systems, and the real implementation of the pay yourself first system. We could use behaviourally optimal strategies of getting workers to commit to positive financial savings budgeting behaviour before they even receive the money written directly into their contracts, a worker could elect to have X percentage of whatever they earn for their entire working life put aside for themselves in a smart pension system, with the increase in financial technology one would never lose pensions again. We could go even further. WeBank, China's first online bank, provides credit analysis based on social media activity online purchase patterns. A worker completing microtasks and receiving remuneration via smart contracts could find considerable benefits, replacing the costs of traditional self-employment. One of the interesting applications of smart contracts, which may need further exploration with regards to its effects on our tax and welfare system, this is of course remuneration doesn't necessarily need to be enough for that is recognisable as money. Smart contracts will have the flexibility to offer alternative forms of reward, an organisation's products or discounts or loyalty schemes, online processing power, storage space or virtual rewards used in online activities. From a tax perspective what exactly is the value of an online expansion pack, upgrading your avatar with a new costume? I'm not sure I have an answer, though I do know that online marketplaces buy and sell rewards, which earned in videogames, often taking many hours of gameplay to achieve, and which are sold for sovereign currency.

We need however, to consider societal, the social, and the behavioural costs (and benefits) of this new approach to work.

CONCLUSION

This chapter begins to imagine a future where the notions of a single primary job are obsolete. We note that the ideas and perceptions of multiple roles are generally that of 'just about managing' with the worker holding down several part-time roles as they are unable to find full-time work. We however speculate that portfolio working will become the norm and that individuals will be able to select work that they want in a competitive, but regulated price marketplace. No worker should be forced to work at below subsistence wages and in deteriorating conditions. However, a review of various work platforms prompts a striking race to the bottom in bidding for work, it is here that the balance between market competitiveness and exploitation requires considerable intervention from the state. If, as we believe the future consists of a large portion of the population working in this manner, wholesale exploitation of the workforce is a possibility without appropriate regulation and measures. As we see further examples of nation states competing for international investment based on lowering worker conditions and wages, as well as reductions in corporation tax, then we must consider where this regulation and protection must come from. It is possible that mass platform use, could drive worker cooperation and enforcement of employment standards and charters, likewise platforms themselves could compete for labour on improved conditions and rates, however one feels that an overall governing body is required to ensure worker rights and conditions.

NOTES

1. https://metro.co.uk/2019/05/07/multinationals-like-facebook-want-to-wrestle-control-of-the-monetary-system-away-from-nation-states-9371329/

2. https://web.mit.edu/simester/Public/Papers/Alwaysleavehome.pdf

3. https://blog.revolut.com/how-the-global-financial-crisis-gave-birth-to-fintech/

4. For example, Financial Services Authority (FSA) (2009).

5. We utilise a description of the correction process as provided by de Soto (2009b). This correction process is however the evolution of 'Austrian thought' and not limited to one author, the works of Hayek and Mises are of particular significance here. De Soto's work is used as he provides a very accessible step by step description of the process. The work of de Soto (2009b) has been widely accepted by the Austrian school, and described by the Mises Institute as 'a complete comprehensive treatise on [Hayekian] economic theory' www.mises.org/resources/2745/Money-Bank-Credit-and-Economic-Cycles, viewed on 9 December 2010.

6. For an explanation of the Ricardo effect, please see: Hayek (1969)

7. It is acknowledged that the broad overview provided here cannot delve into every aspect, for an Hayekian perspective on the global financial institutions please see – International Institutions: seen from the perspective of Austrian Economics, Socher (2009) and for a less objective view; The dinosaur amongst us: the World Bank and its path to extinction, Hooke (2007).

8. de Soto (2010) states that for several years the American money supply has been growing at a rate of over 10% a year whereas before the crisis voluntary saving fell to a negative rate over the corresponding period.

9. In accounting the future money received by a firm or individual is discounted using the interest rate to provide an accounting assumption of its value today, this uses the formula $PV = \dfrac{R_t}{(1+i)^t}$ where PV = the present value, R = future money amount, i = the rate of interest and t = years in the future.

10. Similar to Hayek, Sennholz (1985) is in favour of competition in the production of money, but with state-issued fiat money as well, competition is ensured here with the abolition of legal tender laws.

11. A series of essays on this subject are presented in Salerno (2010).

12. Standard economic analysis terms inflation and deflation as a rise or fall in prices, respectively, Austrian analysis and as used in here refers to inflation as an increase in money and vice versa.

13. Mises sees the rights of private property as a result of human action, a means to an end which like any process can be improved upon, by contrast Hayek (1960) sees private property as an end function of human action, the use of which allowed for market society to triumph over alternatives. Rothbard (1994) develops these views and sees private property as a combination of these ideas.

14. Rothbard (2001) counters three main arguments against deflation within the Austrian school, those that argue falling prices will be damaging to business, deflationary increase in real debt would be detrimental to production and that contraction of credit would worsen a depression. Rothbard's counter arguments can be traced from Mises and Hayek and are evident in contemporary works such as de Soto's (2010) reform proposals.

15. Mises (1966) states how any state intervention in the monetary process can be unwise as un-backed expansion of the money supply can occur to aid the state in times of crisis.

16. For instance, Sennholz in his early works (1955) condemns deflation as an extremely harmful policy, and is a supporter of Mises' anti-deflationary reform proposal; in his later study (1987) he calls for the people to be liberated from inflation and produces a plan for monetary reform that is likely to be severely deflationary (Bagus, 2003).

17. A criticism of the general view of the Austrian school on the removal of the state is that it is simply unrealistic, Zimmerman (2003) states that in the real world there is a high probability that central banks will continue to exist despite Austrian wishes, with the general public perception in light of the recent financial crisis that banking needs in fact closer supervision and state control, this seems extremely likely.

4

THE FUTURE OF WORK: THE EMERGENCE OF THE BITWORKER

INTRODUCTION

In this chapter, we look at how work will evolve to where the idea of a permanent single job is rare and how multiple income streams become the norm. We consider implications for training and education and envisage what work will look like.

EVERYONE IS A SPECIALIST, EVERYDAY COMPETITION FOR EVERY TASK, A RACE TO THE BOTTOM?

We have seen that, in the algorithms, blockchain and cryptocurrency (ABC) economy, work is eventually broken down into its constituent microtasks and that as these tasks become simpler and simpler, the skill set required to do them becomes less. As such, the eventual and inescapable conclusion is that there will be little to no specialisation as we currently recognise it and that virtually any task could be completed by virtually any individual. Complex microtasks can emerge from the ABC economy, but again, they will be broken down to simpler forms.

Surely then, this represents a classic race to the bottom. If any task can be completed by any individual to the same standard, then organisations need to only pay subsistence wages (or less) to get the microtask completed. This assumes though that the power relationships between the organisation and the Bitworker are weighted in favour of the organisation. In a microtask world, with the predicted increase in the volume of microtask, there will be few (if any) microtasks which will be standalone consequential for the Bitworker. In any economy, there are usually more workers than work hours to be completed, in a microtask economy this could very well be the other way around. Microtasks are expected to increase in number following the exponential pattern of the increase in computer power, worker numbers (even in the global ABC economy) following the pattern of human procreation are not expected to match this growth.

There could well be a situation where a worker has a near inexhaustible offer of microtasks to complete and the knowledge that each they do complete has a considerable potential opportunity cost. The power relationships between firms and Bitworkers could favour the Bitworker.

However, a clear issue with any futurist view is the trap of taking notions from our current and assuming that these remain constant, this ABC future may challenge our understanding of what an organisation even is. We could move between dystopian notions of omnicorporations, positive and negative views of global governments coordinating all economic activity, or anything in between. For the purposes of this book, and remembering that the future we are proposing isn't too distant, being the culmination of existing technologies and trends discussed in chapter 1, we need to assume that in terms of organisation the ABC future will look broadly similar to today. In a later chapter, we note that the effect of the ABC economy on national government and regulation may be much more significant than on the organisations, especially organisations which are already hyper-global.

Then, assuming that the idea of organisations stays relatively constant, but the idea of work moves to microtasks, then how does the Bitworker choose work, differentiate themselves and in short, succeed. Of course, in an algorithmic age, with an increasing supply of microtasks of different themes, types and values to the worker, it would in theory be possible to coordinate Bitworkers and Bitwork to allow for the scenario where every worker completes the same number of random microtasks and receives the same reward. Moving away from the idea of a perfectly coordinated economy where all process Bitwork to meet their determined needs and to a scenario where much of the economic infrastructure remains similar to today, then we can make several key assumptions:

1. Organisations (platforms) will develop to match Bitwork to Bitworker.

2. Bitworkers will differentiate themselves, not with skills or specialisms but with attributes.

3. A review or rating system will exist to differentiate Bitworkers.

4. Bitwork will provide a base level of income in society.

5. Other social security or welfare will need to be maintained by governments.

In order to present the societally positive view of Bitwork, we have presented in this book, points 3, 4 and 5 will likely need regulation and policy action. The ratings system needs to be fair, the base level of income needs to be adequate and individual workers who cannot participate in the Bitwork economy need dignified protection.

IS THE ABC DESTRUCTIVE OR COMPLIMENTARY TO WORK?

In order to look at this potential future where algorithms have broken outputs down to fundamental microtasks, where blockchain via smart contracts is providing certainty and security for input and output relationships between organisation and worker, and is providing instantly transparent and verifiable information, and where cryptocurrencies are facilitating global payments, We first need to look into the past. There are striking parallels between the ABC future and the First Industrial Revolution. We note that these discussions are ongoing, but that there are many comparisons between today's age alteration, the current threat to AI and automation policing jobs and activities and the disintermediation potential blockchain. However, throughout this book, we strive to develop a future where the individual technological trends and supertrends have converged and created a potential future greater than the reach of any single technology. We believe that this future can be analysed through the lens of the Industrial Revolution, as a societal, economic and political transformations of work, can in fact in a broadbrush sense, be looked at in some ways is a removal of some of the constraints placed on workers by, in particular, the factory system, and we will argue this in some ways the ABC may represent societal transformation to a world of work with more freedom.

From a historical perspective, the Industrial Revolution was of long-term economic benefit to society. However studies must also consider the long-term environmental effects, and whether some of the benefits accrued owing to the Industrial Revolution, quite simply, were economic output benefits generated from stealing the future. A key consideration is that whilst the Industrial Revolution was undoubtedly long-term economic benefits, the main question of course concerns the short-term effects, Frey (2019) states

> *three generations of working Englishmen were made worse off as technological creativity was allowed to thrive. And those that lost out did not live to see the day of the great enrichment.*

What then, if anything, is short-term protection, or resistance to the ABC to ensure today's workers don't lose out. The history of technological replacements of particularly middle income work tells us that in the short term these effects could be quite catastrophic. The laid off workers, often struggle to replace their traditional skills, with skills they need to compete in the workforce. In the long-term, we have argued that the notion of skills, of specialisms, or even of professions, may be a redundant concept. One of our key arguments of the process of AI, machine learning and algorithms reducing work to its fundamental microtasks, is in fact a diminishing of the skills required to complete them. However, as Frey (2019), points out, Andrew Yang who is running for US President in 2020 notes, that for instance

> *all you need is self driving cars to destabilise society .... We're going to have a million truck drivers out of work 94% male, with an average level of education of high school or one year of college. That's one innovation will be enough to create riots in the streets. And we're about to do the same thing to retail workers, call centre workers, fast-food workers, insurance companies, accounting firms.*

Labour replacing technology has historically been feared, both by workers and the elites. Workers feared for their livelihoods and lifestyles and mass unemployment of workers and subsequent societal unrest. The Industrial Revolution occurred in the UK, when the landed elite was supplemented by the industrial elite, who had much to gain from mechanisation. The long-term economic gains of industrialisation would not necessarily felt that the workers of the Industrial Revolution. In the Industrial Revolution, notions of time, money and work were completely transformed; in Britain in 1770, most of the population could not even conceive of the idea of a factory, let alone working in one, but by 1830 millions of the population did. This societal shift changed the fundamental bedrock of the pre-industrial society, in particular, the idea of time. Prior to industrialisation, a craftsmen worked from home on their own machines and generally sold their outputs at a weekly market. Craftsmen knew there was only one thing to get the job done and they could work when they liked. They often worked long hours but they had total control over it and freedom that came with it. For this work, they earned middle incomes and had a reasonably comfortable traditional lifestyle, very similar to their parents and the generations that came before them. Then came mechanisation of factories, craftsmen simply couldn't compete, factories in Adam Smith's notions of specialisation to rapidly increase output. Craftsmen taking the whole product was not able to compete, for instance weavers in the Industrial Revolution saw, over a 30-year time period, their average wage falling from around 20 Shillings a week to around 5 Shillings. Traditional workers could not make sense of the factory system. They were being paid to work for a certain amount of hours or days, they were being paid for one process and not seeing the output they were creating. Ideas of money transferred from outputs to time, machines ran at constant levels of outputs and so you were paid for keeping the machine going for a certain period of time, again wholly unfamiliar concepts to the craftsmen. Previously, the idea of time was simply an endpoint which craftsmen had to get the output done by, now it was a regimented broken down technical process which resulted in less control, less freedom and less pay. This was a large structural change in society, and society needed to be prepared for the new mechanisation world. Sunday schools developed for the sole purpose of teaching children when to arrive at a particular place at a particular time.

Time was now transformed, as was the idea of money. However, prior to 1750, per capita income globally doubled roughly every 6000 years. Since the Industrial Revolution per capita income doubles every 50. Longer term the Industrial Revolution was beneficial to the workers and society, but in the short term it was not. However, this time around workers can better see the effect of technology on the demand for their labour, the democratic system gives workers a voice today that they were working in the Industrial Revolution. The labour replacing technology is here and is faster and further developing, society is reacting. Andrew Yang is running for president, and a campaign to protect jobs from automation, regulation and policy can be conceptualised as a response to automation, as can presidential success in campaigning to bring jobs back. In 2013, Frey and Osborne found that 47% of American jobs are at high risk of automation, we would suggest that risk increases with every technological development. So, the question we have to ask is will the ABC destroy jobs and will it, for those jobs are destroyed, create replacements?

Here, we have to look at two scenarios: firstly, the journey to what we've been calling the ABC economy and, secondly, life in the ABC economy. As we postulate, that the ABC economy is a whole new structure of economic activity and coordination, we suggest that this culmination will characterise a distinct stage of global economic activity, similar to the capitalist stage we find currently ourselves in.

The journey to the ABC economy will be characterised by widespread disruption and displacement. We are entering a new freeze in the global economy, where big tech is rebuilding, reshaping and redesigning traditional systems. Earlier in the book, we looked at the journey of finance from traditional institutions and notions of finance, to the disruption of FinTech. We can conceptualise this journey to the ABC economy, in much the same way. We see TechFin as the final stage in this system, a new way of coordinating and generating financial activity, which will be replaced by the next systemic development. Likewise, we can conceptualise the journey of our economy, from a traditional capitalist system which innovates and reinvigorate itself, to automated and knowledge-based economy which shares the same foundations, structures and institutions, but with technology making the systems become more efficient, which in turn gets replaced, as technology doesn't simply make existing systems more efficient, but wholly reinvents them. For a short-term journey than, we can learn lessons both from the Industrial Revolution and from much more recent history of automation and industrial decline. We can see how in particular, middle income wages can decline, and how those displaced by new technology, rarely regain the standards of income and security they had. Here of course is one barrier in the way of the eventual ABC economy, in a way that seemed unlikely even a few years ago, automation anxiety has entered the mainstream debate. Technology taxes and support packages for displaced workers are becoming common themes in political dialogues.

It is here that we can seek inspiration from the Luddites, who were (at least not in the beginning) wholly adverse to new technology, they were adverse to a lack of welfare and protections for workers displaced by it. On the journey to the ABC economy, significant protections are required for labour, to prevent a repetition of that earlier Frey quote, that on the journey to the societally distributed (though of course not equally) economic benefits of industrialisation, one, two, three or more generations of workers are not worse off. These protections, including improved welfare, potentially universal income and advanced and dynamic lifelong learning are discussed in the later chapters. Here we see great potential in new technology redesigning the world of work, the journey to get there without government intervention and policy protections could be comparable to a negative journey of workers in the Industrial Revolution. We hope that this book provides a guide both for workers and policy how to mitigate this.

The next economic stage, that we are terming the ABC economy, can provide in terms of economic growth and income the same benefits that the Industrial Revolution provided to workers a century hence. It is useful when thinking about what this stage could look like, to again take inspiration from the past. In the coming sections, we will propose our idea of a worker in this new economy, and what their economic lives and society may look like.

TRAINING, PAY AND REWARD IN THE ABC WORLD

So then, in this new world ABC is transforming the way we work, where work is broken down to microtasks, with blockchain providing a platform for verifiable transparent information and corporate-cryptocurrencies meaning that we can accept payments for work from hyper-global organisations, with borderless, real time and infinitely divisible instant transactions. We can see that this is a future where the world of work could look very different. If our existing notions of long-term employment, if not a job for life, with specialisms or skills that we trade for income, our human and social capital are all fluid ideas, how does one prepare for a world where work is constantly changing where the microtask you may be adept or highly skilled at disappears. Where the ideas of machine learning, big data and advanced analytics take our successful completion of a task process and replicate that successful completion and replicate the required skill set. What then does the worker in the ABC economy do to prepare to train? Ultimately, we need to examine the very notions of education, schooling, training, Further Education, Higher Education and developing proficiencies in one or two complementary areas and look further towards fundamental skill sets that can be used in the completion of a large range of processes and tasks. Total flexibility and adaptability is required to provide the outputs needed in the ABC economy, but the fundamental question is how to prepare a workforce for this. Instead of training programmes, schooling or university degrees in each of the themes we discussed earlier, it may be instead of becoming a composer, or an architect, or a web designer, one simply becomes a creative. Somebody specialising in coding, or accountancy, or banking, do they become a technical and so likewise, do the workers in the physical sphere simply train their bodies to become as close to autonomous production styles as possible? This will probably be required where the human physicality needs to complement and suit a range of autonomous microtasks. One can imagine a future where the ability of a physical worker to match their approaches to algorithms would be highly prized.

When we look at education and training, one of the big diversions from today is in terms of skill development. We postulate a considerable change in the post-school education, for advanced training, undergraduate degrees, master's degrees, or even PhDs. We see a significant evolution in the microcourse and Massive Open Online Courses (MOOC)-type sphere.

For example, a worker looking at creative work may do free courses or a microcourse of values of an organisation, which would then qualify them to complete microtasks for that organisation. A car production firm, when wanting microtasks completed to support the advertising of their latest product, may require creative microtask completed within the attributes of that firm or for general car selling, that may in turn require a bit worker to undertake a significant amount of online courses. This training, one would expect, following the pattern of the ABC economy to reduce processes down to fundamentals, would be quick and concise, and designed to provide the human with the skills the algorithm needs. Potentially, with a nod to the system and structure we currently have, enough microtask training could accredit someone as a BA (Hons) Creative, BSc (Hons) Technical, etc.

THE BITWORKER

In this final section of this chapter, we discuss our personification of a worker in the ABC economy, a worker that we call the Bitworker, and one that positively interacts with the technological, online and economy. We wish to make it clear that we are not prophesying things or predicting the future. The ABC economy and the bit worker within it are, we think, possible futures, or possible scenarios. It is a fool's errand to make direct predictions, the one prediction we can relatively confident of is that the future as presented in this book, will not look exactly like our writings. We are aiming to give an idea of the future of work and the future of working in a heavily automated, artificial intelligence (AI), algorithmically driven and Blockchain supported future. We hope scholars and practitioners and future workers themselves will continue to explore the themes presented. This is not the precise future, or even necessarily a probable one, we have looked at many aspects of regulation, policy and adaption to this technology, which will be required to provide a future similar to what we present. Even when we proposed this book, the development of technology has continued to outpace government and regulation. We can see anxiety around automation entering into the mainstream political debate, workers' worry for their livelihoods is entering into the political discourse. Their arguments being presented around the nationalisation of large firms, to protect them (or to protect the worker) from further automation, proposes that taxes on robotics, popular warnings against the destructive potential of AI (both in the traditional sense and the employment sense), an unexpected election and referenda outcomes, which can be traced back to the correct idea of those left behind politically and economically, but primarily by the middle income lifestyle, being replaced by automation. The political will, protections and support, we have argued unnecessary to turn what we have termed the ABC economy, into their benefit for all, were not present in these communities or happenings. Workers displaced by automation, and an increasing pace in technological developments, were not offered sufficient welfare, credible training to regain skills to enter the new workplace or even psychological support. Workers in the left behind areas and industries rarely regained what they lost. In our future, we are suggesting displacements on a massive scale, and policy consideration needs to be given to ensure that the potential upside for all, this technological development, is not squandered. It is all too easy, too. The future where increasing automation (at least in the short term) gives rise to greater profitability and greater inequality.

In order to convince the reader that the ABC is more than a revolution of the economy as we know it, we must explore the argument that the ABC is an institutional technology, or convergence of institutional technologies, that the ABC is actually a new way of generating and coordinating economic output and activity. This simply means the ABC is wholly a new type of economic structure and not simply a production exchange efficiency improvement, this is a whole new economic structure, not simply improvements to the structure which we currently inhabit.

The world of work with the future could be structurally, societally, politically, organisationally and economically wholly different to today. It is very hard to imagine a different future and not simply a change of an extension to the present. We argue that the ultimate end of the ABC supertrends is a world of work where worker from today, where they transported into it, would find little familiarity. We hope to position this book in opposition to Amara's Law, where the effects of new technology are overestimated (hype) in the short run and underestimated in the long run. We are taking a long position on the effects of algorithms, blockchain and critical which attempts to see past their current type and look at their long-term effects, in particular the long-term effects of their convergence.

> *Our argument is that until 2009, the economic institutions of capitalism consisted – in the con joint schemas of Hayek, Williamson, Buchanan, North and Ostrom – of firms, markets, Commons, clubs, relational contracts and governments, and that these institutions collectively furnish money, war, property rights, contract and finance through organisations and networks of production exchange (Hodgson, 2015). But since 2009, there has been*

> *an additional mechanism for groups of people to*
> *coordinate their economic activity, i.e. through*
> *the institutional mechanism of a block chain.*
> *(Davidson, De Filippi, & Potts, 2018, p. 641)*

In many ways, our proposal for the ABC economy demonstrates post-industrial structures being replaced by new technological ones. Returning to our analogy from finance and banking, of (1) traditional institutions, moving to a (2) FinTech system which in turn moves to (3) a TechFin system. Remember crucially, whilst the aims of one and three are the same, the structures and processes and operations of three are unrecognisable to one. If we consider the post-Industrial Revolution to structure of economic output to akin to stage I, that is the traditional financial institution, we can see that, the stage roughly from 1967 (with the launch of the first handheld calculator, and thus the precursor to today's smart phone) to the near future. Stage II is that of FinTech, where often significant technological innovations are driving efficiencies and productivity in broadly the traditional institutions structure. Then we can postulate a future stage akin to TechFin, which results in a potential future characteristics not dissimilar to those described in this book. Of course, the journey of activity is dynamic, and we are not suggesting that our TechFin stage is the last one, this will probably be a continual journey based around the circular pattern of traditional institution, technological efficiency to that system, and then fundamental structural developments occurring to produce a new system of output, activity and coordination.

If, as seems reasonable we are moving from stage 2 to stage 3, then we need to look at a short- and long-term evolution of the worker. We are calling our worker, who generate output in the final TechFin comparator stage, the Bitworker and we shall return to examining this worker in a little while.

CONCLUSION

This chapter imagines the future of work from the perspective of the worker, or as we term them, the 'Bitworker', in this new global economy. We use the phrase global economy as we believe that, with a small number of geographic and physical barriers, this new platform-based way of working, will be as global as we can conceptualise. The sellers of online work, the organisations, governments and cooperatives of the future could, in effect, be located anywhere or nowhere and be online entities with zero physical infrastructure or human infrastructure, a further headache for the state and a huge consideration for future research. In effect, a Bitworker in the UK could be working for anyone, and ultimately we doubt they will even know who they are, with trust in the platform, facilitated by blockchain smart contracts and globally acceptable cryptocurrencies, supporting this. The technological infrastructure to support this way of working, already exists; blockchain and cryptocurrency simply make it easier to do. In a world where the process to produce an output or service is reduced to its component or fundamental process, it is a reasonable judgement that the skill set required to produce this output decreases (as the number of microtasks increases). This is the specialisation of which we are already familiar but sped up and ruthlessly efficient. This chapter explores how in a world where skill need decreases, a worker is still able to thrive and differentiate themselves. We draw parallels with the wholesale changes from pre-industrial to industrial worker and query if in some ways the ABC marks a return to a quasi-pre-industrial style of working.

5

PROFIT AND POWER IN THE BITWORKER WORLD

INTRODUCTION

This chapter considers the rise of the Bitworker from the perspective of the organisation. We investigate where the power dynamics play out, consider a tier structure of Bitworkers and ultimately examine where profit flows to – the Bitworker or the organisation.

GETTING WORK DONE, HIRING THE BITWORKER

The Bitworker is a technology-enabled individual bearing the risks and rewards of self-employability at the expense of job security and the guaranteed availability of short to medium term paid work. Similar to the previously discussed platform businesses, we predict the increase in the usage of such business structures looking to connect the availability of Bitworkers with the skill shortages and potential providers of both work and consequential payment. Matching of this human resource may take place using a blockchain system which is able to connect mutually interested parties without the need for a centralised trusted arbiter.

These blockchain labour exchanges may be organised along geographic, professional or other such variables, whereby a worker may seek to advertise their availability across multiple blockchain exchanges concurrently subject to the rules of membership of each respective blockchain. Expanding upon the *digital cooperative* (DCOP) proposed in Chapter 2, such labour exchanges may become not-for-profit vehicles sponsored by the state, regions, trade professions or even by private corporations. In contrast, it is feasible to envisage profit seeking alternatives which purport to provide superior or more exclusive opportunities in return for a larger membership fee which could accrue to shareholder, members or a mixture of both.

In the absence of a centralised arbiter, such exchanges could be termed a decentralised exchange (DEX), which is relatively a new technology that seeks to mitigate the risk of mistrust and misdemeanour by a centralised body. DEXs permit peer-to-peer exchange of value. Presently, they are almost exclusively used for the trading of cryptocurrencies. One such example is Ether Delta whose founder made settlement with the Securities and Exchange Committee for allegedly operating an unregistered exchange.

Recruitment of appropriately qualified and reputable Bitwork professionals would likely involve significant *Know Your Client* (KYC) vetting. This would become increasingly important for safety critical professions requiring such surety and perhaps even full transparency for the respective regulators, where it was in the interest of the public and wider society. The underlying blockchain technology, although just a variant of a database, lends itself well to such a matching process (of labour) which requires real-time access for multiple stakeholders recorded in an immutable audit trail.[1] It is this audit trail which will offer transparency to current and potential members (Bitworkers) and potential contract hirers. Essentially, a system delivers trust from mistrust. However, with the absence of a centralised arbiter, a decentralised financial (or *DeFin*) solution will be required to maintain the accuracy and robustness of this ledger, or audit trail. It is possible that this could be done using a decentralised mining pool of validating nodes, similar to that of Bitcoin, leaving the labour exchange exposed only to a 51% attack from a targeted hack perhaps through the use of quantum computing technology.[2]

For tax authorities such as HMRC in the UK and the IRS in the USA, the existence of pseudo-anonymous systems, such as Bitcoin, and the existence of blockchain-enabled communities which permit users to transfer value outside of existing regulatory structures pose a headache to say the least. It is therefore possible that such *decentralised labour exchanges* (DLEXs) will require authorisation from arbiters such as national and international regulators. Following on from this reasoning, it is plausible that such *DEX* permissions will be preconditioned by the veil of anonymity or pseudo-anonymity being lifted to mitigate the risk of tax evasion with respect to consequential work obtained and performed in this manner. From August 2019, the IRS and HMRC are engaged in contacting individuals suspected of failing to declare their historical gains from cryptocurrency trading. Many believe that such an agenda is impossible given the pseudo-anonymous nature of the technology. However, forced disclosure of KYC information held by cryptocurrency exchanges is facilitating this effort by tax authorities. Much of this may be a public relations strategy rather than a meaningful attempt to claw back hitherto untaxed gains from the shadow economy but nonetheless must be a consideration in our evaluation of the future viability for DEXs of labour.

As with all exchanges there must be some predefined standardisation in terms of contract sizes and durations, etc. This is the case currently for precious metal exchanges such as The New York Mercantile Exchange and COMEX, the equivalent for commodities. For our hypothesised labour exchange, a common unit of work would need to be predefined. This may be a previously discussed *Bit task*, a unit of chargeable time (e.g. an hour/day/week), or a predefined project which itself may be bespoke in nature. Much of the nature of standardisation will depend upon the skill level of workers and the needs of potential contract hire firms. Furthermore, the transparency and trust afforded by the blockchain infrastructure would give a potential contract hire firm full visibility to the concurrent workload for an individual worker both historically and at the present time. This could potentially also include worker reviews and endorsements, not too dissimilar to a LinkedIn plus type system, which thereby becomes an immutable CV to better aid evaluation and hiring. Indeed, future work or contract commitments by worker or provider of work could be made available too where appropriate.

Digital professions such as author, marketer or computer programmer obviously would lend themselves more easily to the above compared to physical or contact-oriented professions, such as builder, teacher or care work. This is not to say that the latter professions could not be efficiently allocated using a DLEX but that their units of time would likely be broken down into larger chunks, for example, six-month short-term contracts in contrast to Bit tasks of the digital worker. These latter digital professions are also more ably suited to a global audience which would mean that a citizen in Thailand can feasibly source work concurrently from organisations in Estonia, Mexico and India. Moreover, such individuals would now be more flexible in terms of their own physical location and tax domicile akin to the *digital nomad* trend that has recently come to the fore.

A digital nomad is a person who is location independent who oftentimes works in technology-oriented industries. The management buy-out (MBO) Partners *State of Independence in America* (2018) identified that an estimated 17 million US workers have aspirations to become digital nomads whilst some 4.8 million Americans already do so. Experts predict that by 2035 the number of digital nomads globally will number in excess of one billion workers. With numbers predicted to rise in the USA and beyond organisations such as WeWork have been established and look well placed to capitalise on this. WeWork is a community for such digital nomads offering infrastructural support for their individual worker needs including shared office space and private accommodation thus enabling a single person business unit or *individual Strategic Business Unit*. Governments have not been slow to react to such trends with Estonia now offering the world's first digital nomad visa which could attract some 1,400 workers per year according to the e-Estonia government agency. According to marketinspector.co.uk (2019), the most common digital nomad professions currently include:

- Software developer
- Translator
- Graphic designer
- Content editor/writer
- Virtual personal assistant
- Search Engine Optimisation (SEO) specialist
- Drop shipper
- Coaching/consultancy.

The *work from anywhere* trend looks to have traction that will be further emboldened by the technology of our triumvirate.

However, it is clear that such flexibility of work would not be suitable for all professions and demographics. It is this suitability that at the point of hiring can be more readily evaluated using artificial intelligence (AI) techniques. Presently, some leading US recruitment companies use AI to digest approximately 25,000 attributes of a candidate interview video before they are matched to potential employers. Variables such as eye contact and speech intonation are all used as markers to identify likely traits and qualities, or lack thereof. It must be stressed that this is technology that although bleeding edge is already here now rather than some envisaged future possibility. Moreover, in the UK organisations such as Red Wigwam, although more people oriented in their evaluation of temporary candidate workers, also employs AI to match workers to employers for contracts of between 15 minutes and 3 months in duration. A movement towards ever decreasing task durations as our predicted Bitworker and Bit task economy becomes manifest.

THIS NEED NOT BE A DYSTOPIA, THE PROS FOR THE BITWORK

The post-gig economy that we hypothesise represents key challenges regarding career choices, worker flexibility, the availability of work and the lack of a secure and reliable income stream. However, as with the majority of technological changes, there are likely to be opportunities for improvements as well as such threats. This has been the case with the aeroplane, the internet and electricity to name a few technological innovations.

A common cause of SME failure is low-quality earnings. That is to say weak or negative cash flow despite reasonable levels of profitability. This thinking is clearly understood by present day sole traders and independent contractors the world over giving rise to key phrases such as 'cash is king' and 'it's not a sale until the customer has paid'. Many solutions in the current economy exist to mitigate these risks. Examples include invoice discounting and factoring which involves the sale of a company's debts, or sales ledger, at an amount less than the gross sale figure in return for immediate cash. This can be an expensive source of financing the negative working capital requirement as a company grows and can typically cost between 5% and 15% of the gross sale depending upon the industry, quality of the debtors (receivables) and whether the arrangement is on a recourse or non-recourse basis.

This begs the question of how this phenomenon may be disrupted by our triumvirate. One such potential solution will be the application of a more advanced type of smart contract which we previously discussed. Such smart contracts can be created to permit the transfer of funds between individuals (their wallets), between an individual and a smart contract or finally, perhaps between two smart contracts. The funds that may vest in this manner between transferor and transferee are typically The European Research Council (ERC) 20 tokens on the Ethereum blockchain which is the industry standard for hosting such smart contracts. These contracts can hold cryptocurrency funds between two counterparties at the inception of a sale or trade which will then be automatically transferred subject to certain condition(s) being met.

Perhaps most simply, the condition can be one of a time constraint in line with the conditions of sale or purchase agreed, for example, 90 days after date of invoice. However, alternatives do exist such as approval by both parties, or even approval by an additional third party. Similarly, AI and oracles can be used to validate that a particular event has occurred in order to release funds based upon external data sources. If it can be imagined and coded then it is possible. The advantage may not be immediately obvious but in a hard coded world where money is paid exactly when it should be there is no delay in payments being made, no money lost in chasing bad debts and businesses is consequently more likely to succeed subject to their cash forecasting calculations being correct. An improvement on the current escrow account that there is no need for a third-party custodian as this role is now fulfilled more cheaply and accurately by an impartial smart contract. Moreover, this can now be a viable approach on a much smaller scale owing to the vastly reduced costs by comparison. Expanding this out on a macro-scale, we envisage a world with greater employment through more companies succeeding where previously they may have failed. Trust is improved, uncertainty reduced and the cost of capital falls thereby increasing the likelihood of investment which drives growth and employment further.

It should however be noted that this is not good news for all. Financial services companies are likely to see significant disruption as this friction is removed from our business to business (B2B) supply chains, including bridge financiers, custodians and providers of revolving credit facilities, etc.[3] Furthermore, legal services may be detrimentally effected in the areas of international trade and dispute resolution.

The benefits of Bitwork will not be limited to cash flow management associated with trade supported by the use of smart contracts and oracle-assisted locks. We also predict potential advancement in the provision of personal finance, particularly in the payday loan and traditional term loan industries. Payday loans came to the fore in the 1990s and have gone on to become significant industries the world over, where permitted by legal, regulatory and religious restrictions. The largest markets globally include; USA, Netherlands, UK, Canada and Australia. Typified by moderate to small loan provisions over very short periods, the loans are charged at aggressive rates of interest, sometimes many thousands of percent per annum. Often expensive and poor value for a demographic of society with little choice to obtain finance elsewhere. Legislation has therefore sought to protect their vulnerability, for example, in the UK in 2014, interest rates on such loans were capped at 0.8% per day by the regulator, The Financial Conduct Authority. In contrast, the Netherlands limited this to 12% over the base rate whereas Australia chose 4% per month which equates to just over 60% per annum under the effect of that cruel mistress, compound interest.

Large payday loan providers such as Wonga in the UK have offered workers with poor credit ratings a bridge on their future earnings from paycheque to paycheque in a more structured and legal way at rates preferable to the eyewatering charges levied by loan sharks.[4] Further disruption may be possible in this space for the benefit of the Bitworker in the form of microsecuritisations offered by cryptocurrencies such as MAKR's © DAI stablecoin or token administered through their DAO.[5,6] A single DAI coin is backed by Ethereum and is pegged to one US dollar which has been relatively stable, as is the intention, over time since its inception in 2017. The peg is administered in a decentralised manner on the Maker Dao's platform where users can deposit their Ethereum within a bespoke collateralised debt positions (CDPs) in return for DAI coins to the value of the underlying Ethereum less a haircut. Similar to that of a pawnbroking arrangement, the user still has the rights to the underlying Ethereum and can at any point during the life of the CDP redeem the Ethereum by returning the DAI coins originally issued. This permits the volatility of Ethereum to be traded away for the stability of the DAI coin without giving up the upside potential of the underlying Ethereum price movements. In contrast, should the price of the underlying Ethereum fall beyond the buffer of the aforementioned haircut then the CDP is automatically liquidated in order to preserve the integrity of the one DAI to one US dollar peg. An innovative piece of decentralised financial engineering which vastly reduces the scale requirement of the securitisation industry which historically has required under-lying asset values in the hundreds of millions of dollars to warrant the expense of establishment and maintenance. This industry has typically focussed on large illiquid assets such as unsecured loan pools, real estate (*real estate investment* trusts) and mortgage books of business. MAKR © have out-lined a desire to open this structure up to other types of assets including Bitcoin and gold. Organisations offer above mar-ket rate remuneration to buy up future time of individuals, in substance a short/medium term contract of employment.

However, we would not limit things there. It may become possible for Bitworkers to securitise their future time in the format of smart contracts within CDPs. Similarly, this would then allow Bitworkers to monetise their future selves and draw down on that today in the form of DAI (stablecoin cryptocurrency) thereby effectively serving as a payday, or even term, loan. Owing to the decentralised nature of this structure, more reasonable rates of interest would be possi-ble to the advantage of the Bitworker. However, challenges would ensue regarding the intangible nature of the asset backing regarding contingency failure to make good on the securitised future time as well as how to price and gain com-fort over the different earning rates of competing Bitworkers.

HOW WILL AN ORGANISATION NEED TO ADAPT?

The challenges for organisations and the way they recruit, train, remunerate and manage will be both significant and pervasive across their internal divisions. Human resource (HR) depart-ments are likely to require a significant uptick in their techno-logical abilities in order that they mirror the changes observed externally as the fourth industrial revolution manifests.

As previously discussed, trend towards independent contractors rather than employed workers begins to take hold
the organisation of the future will need to become more efficient at locating and sourcing their skill needs from this more
fluid pool of Bitworkers, who are now potentially available
via DLEXs. Decisions will need to be made on the number
of Bit tasks required as well as desired ratings, any physical location requirements and the process of managing work
output in terms of both quality and completion. The surety
of a blockchain infrastructure may be appropriate here given
the comfort of immutability and real-time access required
from a number of interested stakeholders. A kind of verifiable
LinkedIn which sources your current and future work but
without the need for LinkedIn as a centralised and trusted
arbiter. The HR departments of the future will likely require
a greater technological awareness to navigate these new
waters but also may go further and use AI-enabled oracles
to automatically source workers in a bid to outperform their
competitors. Perhaps one day we may even see strategic shifts
whereby supermarkets such as Tesco who engage in *landbanking* also undertaking a *timebanking* strategy to buy up
large quantities of time of particular skill sets and professions
akin to an aggressive retainer-type structure used by legal and
accounting professionals.[7]

Remuneration and benefits may also see significant changes.
Owing to near costless transactions using cryptocurrencies,
we are likely to see the frequency of payments increased
significantly from weekly or monthly to near real-time
contemporaneous production, consumption and payment of
goods and services. This is possible due to the enabling of
microtransactions using cryptocurrencies on a decentralised
blockchain platform. See the next chapter for a full discussion
of the macroeconomic impact of this occurrence in the
Internet of Things economy. Furthermore, to be employed, or

tenured, may become the exception rather than the rule where the former becomes almost a badge of honour to signify your superior quality as a worker relative to that of the contract hires employed on short-term contracts of assigned to Bit tasks. According to the US Department for Educational Statistics, about two thirds of college teachers are tenured. Left unchecked our triumvirate technologies would suggest that such numbers would decrease going forward if left unchecked by the resistance of trade unions, legislation and the theorised DCOPs, discussed in Chapter 2.

Financially, the technology-enabled shift from employed to contract workers will reduce the operational gearing of an organisation, that is to say the proportion of fixed to variable costs. In doing so, this reduction reduces the volatility, and therefore risk, in generating future earnings for the benefit of debtholders and equity investors in the form of interest and dividends, respectively. Once again this reduction of risk will lower the cost of finance and allow the organisation to generate superior returns going forward and also more ably to attract external finance to fund growth. Although initially attractive the substance of this change is that risk is being transferred from corporation to workers who no longer have the security of longer term earnings and the availability of work. Instead, if again left unchecked, this plunges their skills and ability to earn at the mercy of the free market which will be welcomed by some with scare skills and a more flexible lifestyle and commitments but will heap uncertainty, doubt and pressure on to your average working family with 2.4 children. Industries where the employers will benefit more readily from this predicted change will be those where a larger proportion of their cost base is composed of personnel cost – examples include: banking, education and consulting.

Notwithstanding the above detrimental impacts to the worker of the future, the power of choice of work and physical domicile accrues to the worker. The organisations of the future must therefore adapt to align their talent resourcing accordingly. Perhaps most challengingly will be how such workers of the future will be managed and their interests aligned with that of the organisation. It has long been understood that a problem of agency, known as *agency theory* exists to between the misalignment of interests between directors and shareholders. Perhaps more worryingly a greater misalignment, at least in aggregate, may now exist between shareholders and their increasingly fragmented Bitworker labour force. Such workers may be working concurrently across multiple employers raising concerns for employers around commercial sensitivity and competitiveness as well as the risk that a different employer is being prioritised at your expense in the Bitworker's work portfolio. Moreover, such Bitworkers will be engaged in microtasks or Bit tasks which by definition will be short term in duration. These workers will then be spending time sourcing future engagements before their present engagement concludes perhaps to the detriment of their work effort, which you are paying for. Such Bitworkers are likely to be temporally sensitive in that they prioritise decisions and project implementation which either increases the likelihood of being hired again going forward or perhaps ensuring that gains and favourable feedback accrue to them in the short term rather than a different Bitworker further down the line. Regardless, such sub-optimal decision making, although rational for the Bitworker, is detrimental to shareholder interests. Famous examples of such myopia leading to poor decision making by Directors include the ponzi schemes of Bernie Maddoff and the regulatory and accounting breaches of Enron leading to a jail sentence and an ultimate corporate collapse, respectively. These agency problems are however less frequent as the actions of board directors are heavily scrutinised by analysts and the wider markets, particularly for larger listed organisations. We do however note the trend towards, relatively inconsequential fines for wrong doing, where an organisation accepts an initial fine rather than face further investigation. In effect they have the ability to buy off scrutiny. This is compounded by the 'newness' of, particularly data and privacy scandals. The law here is still evolving and legal definitions of a crime lag behind societal ones. It is interesting to note how consumer and societal action can have a far greater effect on moderating and limiting negative organisational behaviours than legal or regulatory pressure. The unique challenge of the agency problem at the Bitworker level, termed *operational agency theory* (OAT), is that for a single worker it is much smaller scale and therefore more difficult to identify, not to mention manage and correct for. Importantly though, the aggregate effect of such agent-based failings may be greater than that of traditional agency theory at board level thereby acting as a sustained drag on corporate performance. This hypothesised OAT drag may serve as a natural brake on the fragmentation of the labour force thereby incentivising organisations to maintain a larger proportion of permanent employed workers than they might otherwise choose to do so going forward.

A further way which organisations may manage Bitworkers in the future is with the use of derivatives.[8] The future availability and price of skills procured sourced via DLEXs would become a significant risk factor for many organisations. Where new risk occurs financial engineering and secondary markets soon follow thereby facilitating the repackaging and sale of risk between parties who do not wish to suffer it compared to those that will in return for a fee. The consequential creation of derivatives denominated in worker time by profession is then entirely possible. The purchase of a futures contract on 10,000 hours of solicitor time at a rate of £300.00 per hour during quarter one 2020 in the Northwest of the UK is possible and of clear commercial value to a large law firm in Manchester such as DLA Piper or Eversheds Sutherland (International).[9] In contrast, a call option on 4,000 mining hours in Western Australia during the next fiscal year for a rate of AUD$ 100.00 per hour would be of interest to the likes of BHP Billiton or Rio Tinto.[10] Invariably, speculators would follow who would trade labour by profession and regions owing to shifting local, regional and macroeconomic needs although it may be some time before we see labour desks on the trading floor of leading investment banks such as Goldman Sachs. Perhaps more likely would be the emergence of exclusion or block-out provisions which would give comfort to employers whilst compensating workers who allow them to dominate their time. A potential win-win for both parties but a provision which is likely only to be afforded to the more highly skilled professions and those where previous employer feedback and ratings are particularly high. This may put further pressure on the disaffected areas of our global societies who perceive, and arguably have been, left behind and failed to have a fair share in the benefits of globalisation.

PROFIT AND POWER IN THE BITWORK WORLD

The systems of soft and hard power will be fractured and redistributed in the future world of work, enabled by our triumvirate. As previously discussed, this is unlikely to be in a uniform manner but rather will vary depending upon industries, regulation, skill levels and availability of current and future pools of labour. However, what is clear is that we envisage a post-gig economy where risk is transferred from corporates to individual workers. We see a resurgence of trade union power using DCOPs as individual workers become further isolated as economic units to be efficiently allocated but ironically are able to use these decentralised financial tools in order to pool their interests and thereby share the risks and rewards of working in isolation. Invariably, hierarchical for-profit labour exchanges may evolve as second-order effect if they are founded by individuals of influence who are able to obtain large contracts from multinationals and then offer them to members of their labour exchange akin to a present day recruitment company.

Nonetheless, some of the largest global employers are unlikely to be exclusively at the mercy of such DLEXs or even their for-profit equivalents. Instead, we may see the leaders within particular industries creating their own exchanges and mandating that they will only resource from these pools of labour. This may include: McKinsey's (Consulting), Google (Tech), Tesla (Next Gen Automotive), etc. This tension could be a grab for power with tension existing between individual workers, employers and private enterprise (the middlemen). With employers such as Walmart (2.3 million workers), The National Health Service (1.7 million workers) and The China National petroleum Corporation (1.6 million workers), it would be a reasonable position to envisage that some, or most, of the power and consequential benefits will accrue to multinationals. A further brake to this trend of hyper-globalisation is the role of the state and global trading blocks which hitherto we have not fully explored.

Similar to the disparate reaction to cryptocurrencies over the previous decade, a similarly uneven response may be likely at the state level as different governments interpret the opportunities and threats for their workers and the triumvirate technology impact. This ranges from countries like Switzerland and Estonia who are championing this new technology through to India who have largely banned the trading of cryptocurrencies by example. Overall, the dynamic of power and consequent profit will, and is, split three ways between that of decentralised solutions for the individual (e.g. Bitcoin), the nation state (e.g. Central Bank Digital-issued Currencies) and the corporation (e.g. JP Morgan). Technologically speaking, the minting of new currency is no longer the preserve of a nation state so the continued trend of such corporate-issued non-sovereign currencies is expected.

It is this minting of currency which is where power resides. The desire to control a monetary system allows the controlling nation state or corporate to wield power and influence over its users. Just consider, that some 10% of all global trade is conducted by the USA, yet 50% of all global trade is denominated in the US dollar currency. It is this reliance on the dollar as a global standard which affords the US greater economic and political power since its domestic monetary policy controlled by Government and The Fed will have disproportionate far reaching consequences beyond its borders. The potential therefore exists for an individual to therefore tokenise, or essentially securitise, themselves in order to take this power away from nation states for their own benefit; the *securitised self*.

The mechanics of a global economy with some near eight billion individuals whom have all issued their own bespoke currencies, in themselves, raises many questions of functionality, taxation and legislation to name but a few. Nonetheless, this recognition and trend is already starting today as increasingly small nations begin to explore introducing their own state backed Central Bank Digital Currencys (CBCDs) to run in parallel with their existing adoption of invariably the US dollar. One such example is that of the Marshall Islands who in 2018 passed The Sovereign Currency Act outlining their intention to issue the Marshall Sovereign digital currency based upon blockchain technology and with a fixed supply. The Honourable David Paul – Minister In-Assistance to the President and Environment of the Marshall Islands – explained in 2019 that, 'they

(The Marshall Islands) wanted to be connected to the global financial system on their own terms' and that 'centralized solutions (of money) are not workable in a country of a little over 50,000 people spread across over 1,000 Pacific islands. This can be compared to Congressman Brad Sherman who in May 2019 said that

> *an awful lot of our (U.S.) international power*
> *stems from the fact that the dollar is the standard*
> *unit of international finance and transactions [...]*
> *it is the announced purpose of the supporters of*
> *cryptocurrencies to take that power away from us.*

Nonetheless, this Marshall Islands are still a nation state albeit a small one comparatively. It is therefore in its own gift to mint its own currency, and therefore it could be argued that as a unit of geographic scale this provision can go no further. You would be wrong to think so. City and regional level currencies exist the world over. Here in the UK by example, we have: The Bristol Pound, The Lake District Pound and the Liverpool Pound. In fact, many such examples exist the world over, including but not limited to: Calgary Dollars in Alberta, Equality Dollars in Philadelphia, the Tumin currency in Espinal in Mexico, the TEMs currency in Volos in Greece and Ithaca Hours currency in New York. This fragmentation of currency presents problems of standardisation and therefore utility to the user as currency is an instrument for whom the benefits scale. However, for the worker of tomorrow, their time is their own and therefore in a future world where their monetary worth can be measured and traded in secondary markets via DLEXs what is to stop their respective units of time from being tokenised?

Continuing this thought experiment, perhaps an incremental phase in this trend towards the *securitised self* will be banding of uniform labour units. As previously discussed, this standardisation of labour is essential for the pragmatic pricing and operation of exchanges, and corresponding derivatives where such things may one day be traded.

This is probably a logical point at which to take a step back and take a *helicopter view* as the management consultants would say. Thus far, we have defined many different forms of future money which have broadly wrapped under the umbrella title of *cryptocurrencies*. They are as follows and are depicted over the page as part of the continuing story of the evolution of money (Fig. 2).

Fig. 2 depicts the evolution of money over time both backwards and forward looking. The future of money is split into four ways between: (1) decentralised cryptocurrencies such as Bitcoin; (2) Corporate-issued non-sovereign currencies such as Facebook's Libra; (3) the securitised self – a hypothesised

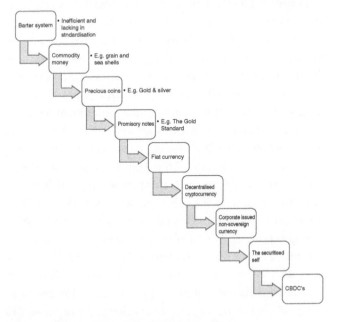

Fig. 2.   The Evolution of Money Over Time.

tokenisation of professional labour time; and (4) CBDCs – central bank-issued digital currencies, for example, the crypto pound. The latter again is a theoretical construct rather than a present reality. This chapter aimed to evaluate the future of money and to whom the gains of monetary policy control would accrue. The four scenarios shown above are not mutually exclusive and in truth it is a difficult call to make in quarter four 2019. For Bitcoin and the other permissionless *alt coins*, we have seen a potential bubble then subsequent decline, but these currencies have yet to dissipate and the reluctance to depart from the plausible future is noted. Alternatively, the corporate-issued non-sovereign coins attract perhaps the most media and political attention, not least in part due to Facebook's Libra. It should however be noted that JP Morgan's institutional currency is effectively the institutional equivalent to Libra's offering to the retail market. A more palatable offering that arguably flies under the radar. In contrast, the securitised self is perhaps the furthest from our present reality. A technological possibility which is consistent with the alignment of the current trend for increasingly short units of time for worker tasks. A concept which we have termed the *Bit task*. Finally, CBDCs represent the institutional repost to the threat of cryptocurrencies such as Bitcoin. Most central banks globally are exploring the mechanics of how such a currency would integrate into the current international economic systems. It is the opinion of these writers that corporates are unlikely to miss this opportunity without a fight. We as global consumers spend directly with corporates rather than governments. The latter tends to be indirect spending via taxation. For this reason, on balance, it is perhaps the corporates who will steal the day and therefore the spoils of what may become the next phase of globalisation. The ability to sell goods and services to consumers along with the monetary system which is used to purchase them. Central bank beware!

NOTES

1. According to PricewaterhouseCoopers Blockchain Fitness Tests (2018).

2. A 51% attack describes a process whereby an individual (or collection of individuals) wield a significant amount of computer processing power. If such power exceeds 51% of the total processing power deployed by the mining community, then a hacker(s) can essentially hack and thereby undermine the principles of a decentralised finance community. On 5th January 2019, the cryptocurrency Ethereum Classic (ETC) suffered such a hack where a single person took control of circa 60% of the community by processing power.

3. Business to business transaction.

4. Under administration since August 2018 being overseen by Grant Thornton UK LLP.

5. A stablecoin is a particular type of cryptocurrency which is asset backed by another asset to overcome price volatility relative to fiat currency or to aid the utility of moving and pricing assets such as gold. Decentralised examples include: the Winklewoss twins Gemini Dollar as well as Paxos and Tether, the latter of which has come under significant pressure from regulators in the USA regarding the strength of their dollar backing. Finally, commercial examples of JP Morgan's JPM Coin (backed by the US dollar on a one-for-one basis) and the recently announced Libra coin by Facebook which will be backed by a basket of world leading fiat currencies and short-term government securities.

6. Decentralised autonomous organisation. A smart contract vehicle often containing value denominated in a cryptocurrency and hosted on a platform such as Ethereum. DAOs are typically given a predefined set or rules or protocol by which funds can be deployed or invested.

7. Landbanking is often used by large retailers to acquire land in ideal locations typically just outside of towns and cities. This is done to ensure that sites are available for future potential growth

of stores but crucially also to inhibit the availability of such land to competitors thereby curtailing their potential for growth.

8. A derivative is a contract which moves in value (up as well as down) with the movement of another variable. Hence, it derives its value from the other variable. Such derivatives can be used to mitigate risk from a hedging strategy with popular derivatives including: commodities, foreign currency exchange, interest rates and stock market indices.

9. A futures contract is a commitment to buy. It is a binding contract.

10. A call option is a contract that gives the holder the right, but not the obligation, to buy a given quantity of the underlying variable for a fixed price on a fixed date. Note that the corollary of this is the put option which is the right to sell.

6

MANAGING THE BITWORKER ECONOMY

INTRODUCTION

This chapter investigates how our understanding of an economy changes in a Bitworker and *Bit task* world. How do our established institutions and Policy Tools work in this world?

Moving away from the Bitworker to now consider the macro-level effects of these disruptive triumvirate technologies, our main concern must be the lack of uniformity in how these benefits are received, perhaps allocated, across societies. The commoditisation of previously skilled and semi-skilled labour may further marginalise many within the ever increasing left-behind who fail to receive the benefits of globalisation and technological enhancements relative to often the incumbent power and educated classes. The consequences for how this may play out in our politics and international affairs would be of concern to us all and arguably not a world within which we would wish to live and work. Indeed, protections must be in place to ensure that workers are not exploited and perhaps more importantly, do not perceive themselves to be exploited.

The tokenisation and market pricing of labour across new technological platforms such as decentralised labour exchanges (DEXs), although efficient, must not proceed unchecked at a macroeconomic level. Such protections at a governmental or regulatory level might include minimum per unit (Bit task) pricing equivalent to a national minimum wage or national living wage. Additional mechanisms may also include restrictions on the amount, or proportion, of time that an individual is permitted to forward sell on these new markets. The objective of such a proposal would be twofold. Firstly, Bitworkers who are in demand would obviously be able to forward sell a larger amount of their future work time, for example, an architect may be able to say seven years of their future work given that she is in high demand whereas an underwriter only two years because comparatively there is less demand or perhaps concern about ultimate job replacement owing to automation.

You would be forgiven for wondering what the problem is with selling your future self. Surely it is a good thing with the future worker? Such an arrangement would provide a guarantee of future income and the provision of work, and with such certainty workers such as the architect above will be able to better plan financially as well as access financial products such as loans and mortgages for a lower fee because they represent a reduced risk given that their future work is guaranteed. This upside must however be contrasted against the status quo of today. The forward contract above is much more restrictive than a contract of employment. Indeed, once committed, should you suffer ill health or perhaps a change of location or career is desired, you would have to compensate the counterparty of the contract who is essentially the person or institution who has purchased your future time. Similar to that of a professional footballer – a five-year contract with Manchester United Football Club is to be celebrated in providing you with certainty of income, but ultimately you are tied to that club for that period of time irrespective of the performance of the team and any changes in your preferred location or club going forward.

Secondly, consideration must be given to the protections afforded to more senior workers under such future market-oriented arrangements. As a future worker approaches retirement, it may be the case that the market prices their work differently compared to that of a senior worker – particularly more physical work where a *Bit task* such as a day of scaffolding maybe priced at a discount by the market owing to the inevitable reduction in physical ability associated with older age which comes to us all. These off market price variations could punitively affect the incomes of our more senior workers, the corollary of which would be discounted younger worker rates, although the later may be more acceptable in a future economy because such workers will be less skilled or experienced.

If derivatives such as futures contracts denominated in worker time become common place then it follows that other financial contracts such as options would come to bear. Unlike a forward contract, an option is the right but not the obligation to buy or sell a quantity of something at a given price (the strike price) on or by a certain date. In our hypothetical future such an option could look like this:

Type of option:	Put (the right to sell)
Quantity:	3,600 hours, equivalent to 37.5 hours pcw over 48 weeks p.a.
Underlying labour:	Solicitor level 4 in conveyancing in Singapore
Other terms:	Tied to a skilled individual or perhaps more likely a pool of such individuals, a digital cooperative (*DCOP*)

Price:	USD 800.00 per day equivalent to 7.5 hours
Exercise when:	Anytime (an American option)
Duration:	Five years from 1 January 2020
Premium price today:	USD 14,500.00
Settlement type:	Cash

The above contract would be bought and sold for a price known as a premium where the seller of the option contract would receive the premium and the buyer of the option would pay the premium. Such a transaction in the secondary markets could be traded and recorded on a decentralised exchange using a blockchain platform, which let us not forget is simply a ledger or database capable of real-time use by multiple stakeholders. Stakeholders interested in the trading of such contracts would be speculators, corporations, trade unions and individuals to name but a few. Simply, speculators have little interest in procuring or selling the future labour but rather they take a view whether this contract is under or overpriced today then trade accordingly. For example, if I believe that demand for solicitors in Singapore will increase going forward owing to my expectation for a buoyant property market over the next half decade then I would also expect the market rate for conveyancing labour to increase with the passage of time. This option contract gives the holder the right to sell such labour for USD 800.00 per day. However, if the labour rate increases to USD 1,000.00 per day then the option is *out of the money* as who would want to sell at USD 800.00 using this option contract when they could sell at USD 1,000.00 in the open market? Consequently, the premium would fall to say USD 6,500.00 to reflect this. A speculator with the above opinions on future market movements would therefore

sell the above put option today for USD 14,500.00 then buy
it back in the future for USD 6,500.00, thereby making an
USD 8,000.00 profit per put option contract. Notice that at
no time does the speculator have any need for the underlying asset – the labour. It should also be understood that the
maximum gain for this short put trade is USD 14,500.00 in
the scenario where the premium falls to a price near nil. However, the maximum loss is potentially infinite and would occur
when demand for such labour plummets allowing holders of
the put option to sell at the guaranteed price of USD 800.00
per day which in turn would make the option contract desirable and the premium would rise.[1]

Individuals and trade unions (or their future equivalents)
would be interested in buying such a put option as it afford
them future income protection. If you were such a conveyancing solicitor in Singapore and you wished to protect your future
income owing to your mortgage repayment obligations, then
the purchase of this option would assist you. Your risk would
be a reduction in your future wage below USD 800.00 per day.
If this occurred, the put option above would be *in the money*
and would allow the holder to sell said labour at a rate which
is now greater than the prevailing market rate. The premium
would increase to reflect this and the solicitor could sell the contract to close their position for a profit which will offset their
employment losses in the real world. The upshot being that they
can now meet their mortgage repayments as they fall due using
both their now reduced employment income alongside their
derivatives trading profit. In summary, this trade has afforded
the worker, or collection of workers, a minimum wage but at
a cost. Insurance always comes at a cost. It seems unlikely that
future *Bitworkers* will become expert in derivatives trading with
respect to their own labour. Perhaps more reasonably such protections will be managed by trade unions or DCOPs, in return
for a fee, on behalf of a pool of workers in a common profession.

Employers too would surely not miss out on the benefits of trading such derivative option contracts. Presently, many corporates engage in hedging strategies to mitigate external price fluctuations of variables (such as commodity prices) which are important to their business operations. This is recorded in their accounts under International Accounting Standard (IAS) 39. It therefore follows that these employers would be keen to manage their often significant employment costs in a similar way. To continue with our example, a legal firm in Singapore would be exposed to increasing wage demands from their staff. They would therefore need to trade the previous put option such that as the wage rate increases they will make money from their derivative trade which will offset their loss in the commercial world. The employing legal firm will therefore sell the put option now for USD 14,500.00. If the wage rate then begins to climb in the commercial world, the put option premium will fall as it will become less desirable to hold. The employer will then buy the put option back to close out their position making said gain.

A well-functioning secondary market for these derivatives would allow trade unions to negotiate pay deals with employers through these disintermediated markets rather than protracted rounds of negotiations, brinkmanship and the potential threat of strike action. Unions could facilitate the sale of blocks of aggregated future labour time for their membership ensuring that they receive the best possible market rate. However, it is questionable whether the marketisation of future labour would enable workers of the future to receive better pay deals using this mechanism. Despite this price (wage rate) uncertainty, the forward sale of future labour would serve as an enhanced retainer system of sorts providing the worker with security that hitherto was not there. However, that does beg the question of what would happen if either counterparty was unable to provide or consume labour? For example, the employer closed their operation and had no need of the future labour, or perhaps the worker wished to move location of careers and therefore was unwilling to make good on their commitment for future labour. In any well-functioning economy such flexibility is required. Provisions would therefore need to be incorporated into the legal terms (or indenture) of such derivatives making provision for such occurrences and perhaps a mechanism for financial compensation in either direction. Leaving prepaid employment early may therefore require the worker to buy themselves out of the contract to which they are presently engaged.

Large corporates compete on the global stage for scarce resources including raw materials, retail space and human resources. It may therefore be the case that in such a world rival employers, and perhaps even nation states may seek to buy up strategically important future labour time in order to profit or even block the development of a competitors business played out and planned using game theory scenario optimisation. Notwithstanding this possibility, the ability to nationalise a current private industry now becomes infinitely more complex. For example, the Labour Party (the official opposition in the UK) have pledged to renationalise the rail system in the UK should they come to power. However, in a world where labour can be traded and forward sold not only would the assets and businesses be required to be bought by the state in a nationalisation process but also any associated future labour time in that industry.

Perhaps more interestingly, this also offers the opportunity for a new hybrid type of nationalisation, namely *nationalisation of labour*. This would involve the state purchasing all future labour available in a given industry deemed to be of national importance. This would allow the political powers of the day to ensure fair wages and conditions which is usually a key driver for nationalisation in the first place.

Critically however, the assets of businesses could remain in private hands and would not be part of the nationalisation process thereby making such an effort cheaper for the state and ergo the taxpayer likewise. In addition, moving industry from state to private hands is often a cumbersome, costly and lengthy process. It is typically a seismic decision made and desired infrequently due to these prohibitive costs and the politically charged opinions on both sides of the debate as to whether an industry belongs in state or private hands. This new *nationalisation of labour* process which we propose is quicker and less prohibitive but also quicker to implement in either direction granting Governments more flexibility in their decisions regarding nationalisation or otherwise.

In a world of increasingly cheap provision of money fuelled by lower for longer strategies of leading central banks, you may have been forgiven for thinking that our debt capacity at the national, corporate and personal levels is nearing, or at, saturation. According to the United Nations (2017) report, total worldwide debt exceeded 300% of GDP compared with a prefinancial crisis measurement 10 years earlier of just 200% of GDP in 2007. Our hypothesised future world of *Bitworkers*, *Bit tasks*, *DCOPs* and *DEXs* all enabled by the technological characteristics of our *triumvirate* may further increase this trend. Growing income security, albeit perhaps at a lower wage rate, will increase the propensity of lenders to lend larger amounts, for longer at cheaper rates. This is due to individuals in particular now having more certainty about their future cash income streams and therefore representing lower risk loan recipients thereby increasing their individual debt capacity further still.

Moreover, with the increasing provision of corporate non-sovereign currencies, the effect at the macro-level and the second-order impact upon the worker may be profound. Arguably, the strategy for such corporates is that in addition to the provision of goods and services to their target customers they will now also provide them with the cryptocurrency monetary system with which their customers can purchase said goods and services. In a joint statement in September 2019 both France and Germany's Finance Ministers reacted strongly explaining that, 'no private entity can claim monetary power, which is inherent to the sovereignty of nations'. Nonetheless, the development of what may become corporate central banks is possible. Moreover, we could see them issuing their own currency backed by fiat currency one-for-one. Then, encourage customers and employees to use it thereby stimulating demand, before removing the asset backing akin to the removal of the gold standard in the previous century to give us the fiat currencies that we use as our functional currencies today. The timing of the tipping point when trust of the corporate exceeds trust of the sovereign nation to facilitate this unpegging would paramount in the success or failure of a non-sovereign currency.

TAXATION OF THE FUTURE WORKER

Changing tack slightly, we must also consider the changing administration and payment of employment taxes for the worker of the future, at both the employer and employee level. Presently, such taxes are typically deducted at source for employed persons with a frequency of weekly or monthly in arrears. The employer is responsible for such deductions as well as the payment of their own employment taxes to the tax authority in aggregate. For self-employed persons, the burden of tax owing and payments to be made falls squarely upon their own shoulders given the absence of an employer. This usually involves an annual or biannual submission, or self-assessment, along with responsibility for such workers to maintain appropriate records to substantiate their tax paid, or not paid as the case may be. Furthermore, documentary evidence to substantiate earnings and tax allowable expenses to reduce profits, and therefore taxes owed, must be retained for many years. In the UK, for example, this is required for seven years. This administrative burden can, and should, be relieved by the virtues of a blockchain ledger which can host data (invoices and receipts), to substantiate both earning and deductions in an immutable form which tax authorities can evaluate with confidence.

The inherent characteristics of blockchain technology may facilitate marked improvements for the state, individual and employer of the future. Primarily, such technologies are excellent at keeping real-time records which are accessible to multiple permissioned users where the historical ledger is immutable to alteration. Clear advantages could be afforded here for the maintenance and administration of supporting invoices for work performed and receipts to substantiate tax allowable cost deductions.

However, it is the blockchain-enabled currencies of the future which perhaps deliver the largest changes in this area of the economy. Irrespective of whether the future of money is cryptocurrencies, corporate currencies, the securitised self or central bank digital currencies (CBDCs), one thing is clear – the continued trend is for cheaper, faster and more transparent transactions. It is this reduction in the cost of transactions to nil or near-nil costs that will enable the previously discussed Internet of Things economy by virtue of the newly found viability for the microtransactions. Such transactions were previously oftentimes crowded out by fees, but in this future scenario, the propensity to spend and earn in smaller discrete units is now possible. If payment is possible in smaller increments of time, it therefore follows that the tendering and allocation of tasks in smaller time units will also perhaps occur.

This further supports the potential for work to be tendered and performed in increasingly small units of time as proposed in our *Bit task* above. Similarly, for taxation, the worker of the future will be remunerated at the microtask and therefore also the microtransaction level. The contemporaneous production, consumption and payment for economic activity remove significant friction from value-added economic activities thereby improving the economy as a whole. Furthermore, the necessity for monthly, quarterly, biannual or annual payments to national tax authorities may no longer be required. Instead, taxation owed will be accrued and paid in real time thereby reducing the bureaucracy of tax accounting and payments, which not least will negate the need for extensive accounting rules in this area regarding the over- or underpayment of tax owed, for example, deferred tax assets and deferred tax liabilities on the balance sheets of corporate entities. These balances are in essence only due to timing differences caused by our technological inefficiencies which in our envisioned future 'world of work' will no longer be evident therefore mitigating the need for an entire accounting standard –IAS 12 Deferred Tax Assets and Liabilities. No mean feat a measure of the potential impact of these new technologies!

VILFREDO PARETO AND THE FUTURE WORKER

From a macro perspective, the future of work that we envisage and have discussed thus far, although not without its challenges, would appear to be one in which workers are technologically enabled, with greater future income security and with less administrative drag. However, this perspective will likely not accrue to all members of society in a uniform manner. As previously discussed, demographics of perhaps older non-professional work activities are perhaps more likely to miss out on these advantages owing to the lower price point, lack of desirability and overall commoditisation of their worker behaviour. At the political level, this will take extreme sensitivity and creativity of policymaking to ensure equity and support in the interests of a cohesive society. Often in nature and economics, we may expect to observe a Pareto Effect here, more commonly known as the 80:20 rule. Founded upon the research of the medieval economist Vilfredo Pareto, he found that 80% of the wealth of a nation might reasonably be expected to be wielded by just 20% of the population. Moving forward, we observe that modern businesses might expect for 80% of their profits to accrue from just 20% of their customer base, or perhaps that they spend 80% of their labour time servicing just 20% of their customers by number. If a *Pareto Effect* is observed in the disruption which is to come in the future of work, it seems unpalatable that any economy could stomach one fifth of their working population being left-behind. The societal disruption would be significant, to say the least, and would add further fuel to the fire behind the rise of angry societies and populism trends the world over. However, should these changes manifest over a generation rather than a much shorter timeframe then becomes more plausible that such changes could creep into normal being in our economy. Similarly, the previously discussed halving of trade union membership over the previous generation discussed earlier demonstrates how significant change can take hold if introduced over a generation rather than a short period of time.

Perhaps one way to ensure equitable treatment during the implementation of the triumvirate is to mirror the technological disruption at the political and central bank level also? However, for us to think of this as an implementation is perhaps somewhat inaccurate. As with all paradigm shifting technological innovations, it is difficult for regulatory powers and nation states to hold their technological adoption at bay. This is especially true for cryptocurrencies which although they have failed to achieve significant adoption they have failed to go away quite simply because the benefits which they bring are too great to warrant their elimination. Although, it should also be noted that to 'get rid' of such cryptocurrencies would present some significant challenges, for example, the use of quantum computing to undermine a decentralised community, convincing global users that there should be no demand for such currencies or perhaps a uniform global electrical switch-off in order to render the underlying blockchain ledger as irreparably damaged. It is for these reasons why it seems likely that cryptocurrencies will be present and therefore have an impact in our future world of work despite the fact that we cannot presently identify which of the non-mutually exclusive forms of possible future money depicted in the previous diagram will ultimately become dominant. The notion of a dominant design or dominant logic is apparent here perhaps more so because we are discussing a standard unit of account based upon technological fundamentals. Historically, our technological evolution has seen the creation of new technologies which bring both good and bad facets from a societal and economic perspective; examples include: the telephone, the internet, electricity and now the algorithms, blockchain and cryptocurrency (ABC) of our triumvirate. Extrapolating this impact at a national and supranational level, we could perhaps envisage a decentralised world bank. This would be transparent by design and would allow the global financial system to form a meta decentralised DCOP to better support the workers of the future at the regional, national and global levels. With a mandate to control inflation and provide full employment where possible we may go further and see the creation of an algorithmic welfare state. Such a welfare system would build upon the seminal work of Wood et al. (2019) who discuss the autonomy and algorithmic control in a global gig economy with a particular focus upon online labour platforms. These labour platforms upon which their study is based are in existence today and seek to match providers of paid work with potential workers. However, at a global level, we might anticipate that such platform solutions may become problematic for two key reasons. Firstly, owing to the fact that such organisations are often for-profit then invariably some of the value which is exchanged between worker and the provider of work will be lost to the private enterprise. If however, such an allocation of labour was performed on the previously discussed DEXs then this value would be retained by the counterparties rather than lost to the platform or website. Furthermore, one might envisage that particularly with semi-skilled and non-skilled labour that there is the propensity for the equilibrium labour rates to disproportionately fall as we perhaps see a race to the bottom in willing labour to be performed at ever lower rates in return for scarce work. Akin to a reverse auction theory and the winner's curse it could be hypothesised that left unchecked then labour at the individual level may lose out in the performance of labour at rates less than their individual marginal utility. Once again, we might perhaps return to the role trade unions and how if such technological frameworks are put in place then our need for such organisations will increase in order to mitigate the race to the bottom risk.

THE WELFARE STATE FOR THE FUTURE WORKER

Extending the theoretical marketisation of labour described above, we might further postulate that the associated welfare might flex in tandem with these labour exchanges, ultimately being controlled by algorithms. The algorithmic welfare state would draw upon many of the principles discussed by

Rosenblat and Stark (2016) to enable verification of worker status and need in terms of whether a welfare payment or support is required. Theoretically, this could be applied in real time and would help to plug the gig economy slack which arguably current and future workers are/will experience. Presently, an agency worker has uncertainty of income by definition but when welfare support is warranted and much needed by the worker it is unable to flex in alignment with the provision of work. Often workers must wait many weeks for welfare systems (and payments!) to catch up oftentimes not due to cash flow reasons but rather overly bureaucratic and old systems which are unable to keep pace with the new economic environment and technologically enhanced norma- tive work denominated in *Bit tasks*. Such a dynamic welfare system would allow the flexibility of work performed and work provision to more ably flourish owing to the reduced hurdles in using such a platform for income provision from the perspective of the worker. If future workers have surety of welfare support during fallow times, even at the Bit task level, then the risk of such work and associated income streams diminishes. A welfare state which is able to algorithmically verify your eligibility for welfare support and pay that in response to small periods of time when work provision is unavailable is technologically possible. In such a world, a future worker may in the course of a single day completed a dozen or so tasks for as many organisations whilst also receiving a 7% welfare support for the 1 hour and 20 minutes during which work was unavailable. The aggregate outcome being a living wage is perhaps met if not exceeded. Further- more, because these welfare payments and Bit task engage- ments would likely be hosted on an immutable underlying blockchain, or similar, then the state can also with confidence levy taxes using similar time increments. If such a system is reliable enough to substantiate welfare payments then it is also reliable enough to warrant income tax deductions at source. A near frictionless system! Larger-scale events could also be verified by oracles and feed into such taxation and welfare cash movements. Example might include: marriage tax allowances, family credit tax support post the birth of a son or daughter or perhaps automatic statutory sick pay when verified to an external system signed-off by a medical doctor. The advantages to such a verifiable and real-time system are evident. However, by virtue of the fact that algorithms will be able to see and therefore evaluate holistically at the Bitworker level it will mean that taxation, for instance, is levied and paid at the appropriate marginal rate even if a worker is drawing income from multiple Bit task engagements concurrently. The worker onus to keep records, declare and pay taxation at fixed time points is therefore removed thereby allowing the worker to earn in a more uniform and predictable manner which reduces risk despite no change in the per annum after tax cash inflows.

THE MULTICURRENCY POST-GIG ECONOMY

In the previous chapters, we proposed multiple possible scenarios for the future of money. Whichever prediction wins out it will be required for workers to become comfortable at managing income streams denominated in multiple currencies whether they be: fiat, cryptocurrencies, CBDCs, non-sovereign corporate currencies or perhaps even currencies denominated in the tokenised self. In managing such currencies, there will be exchange rate risk exposure as invariably the types of currencies agreed upon with respect to the matched work within a crowdwork platform will be varied. Exchange rate risk will be evident for future workers as despite the value of the income hopefully exceeding the value of their outgoings it is likely that the currency mixes will not match perfectly.[2] It may be the case that as part of the allocation process of labour workers are able to stipulate a preferred remuneration currency however what is more likely is that the currency denomination of advertised work will be fixed therefore forcing the worker to bear the risk. A possible solution to this may be the transference of exchange rate risk to the tax authority in that non-fiat currencies could be accepted to settle tax payments. Even if acceptable it should be noted that firstly nation states may be unwilling to allow this as it legitimises the unrecognised currency of earnings potentially to the detriment of their own national fiat currency. Nonetheless, this may not be as outlandish as it first sounds because presently the state of Ohio in the USA permits payment of local taxes by individuals in the form of Bitcoin, and has done so since early 2019.[3] Secondly, taxes may only represent 10–50% of outgoings of an individual depending upon their tax strategy and domicile. It is likely that outgoings will largely be denominated in fiat currency and would typically include: mortgage repayments, utility bills, credit card fees, loans and general spending. Such exchange rate risk could simply be absorbed by the individual or perhaps could be neutralised with an extremely low-cost algorithmic broker who would convert incoming currencies to the required outgoing currencies to create a near perfect match in real time. From the future workers perspective, the notion of exchange rate risk therefore becomes a moot point.

Overall, if managed correctly in a manner where the technology is not curtailed by regulation or legal restriction, the potential advantages for the Bitworker of the macro-economy are significant. Friction is largely removed, taxation and earnings automated, and all are supported by a similarly efficient algorithmic welfare state provision. Nonetheless, it seems unlikely that the incumbent political economic powers will relinquish control in full, and indeed perhaps it would be unwise to do so. A hybrid of our suggestions above may therefore one day become a reality. What is clear presently though is that the gig, and subsequent post-gig, economies are moving faster than our existing systems of taxation, welfare and pension provision can keep pace with. The triumvirate that is our ABCs may assist in calibrating this difference in the economies of the future.

NOTES

1. Market labour price could not fall to less than USD 0.00 per day as such individuals would always require some remuneration for their future labour, therefore the maximum potential loss for the speculators trade cannot be truly infinite.

2. A description of a labour exchange or marketplace for work that is both physical or digital in nature as proposed by Howcroft and Bergvall-Kareborn (2019).

3. The Office of the Ohio Treasurer confirms this but also that a 1% fee will be applied to all such transactions.

7

CONCLUSION, RECOMMENDATIONS AND SURVIVAL GUIDE

Throughout this book we have argued that the combination of algorithms, blockchain and cryptocurrency (ABC) has the potential to fundamentally and wholly change the world of work. Indeed, we argue that our very understanding of the terms work and workplace will be structurally altered by the combinational impact of these technologies and that drawing parallels with the economic, social and political shifts of the Industrial Revolution is both appropriate and necessary for our understanding of the effect of these new technologies. We see a future where work is increasingly specialised into its fundamental components or microtasks, where online working, smart contracts and automation (and further mechanisation) have all but eliminated geographic constraints on work, and corporate cryptocurrencies and central bank digital currencies facilitate a secure but pseudo self-employed global workforce or indeed a global workbank. However, as Frey (2019) convincingly argues, one does not question subsequent generations benefit from the Industrial Revolution albeit in terms of economic growth and living standards, the environmental damage of the subsequent generations living standards, may well prove catastrophic for the next. Yet, Frey notes that the workers transitioning into the Industrial Revolution mode of work and workers within the first stages of the Industrial Revolution were significantly worse off than their predecessors, in terms of overall income, conditions and general living. These workers, in effect, were sacrificed on the alter of progress, and part of this book must look at and recommend a course to attempt to prevent the worker of today (and tomorrow) suffering a similar fate for longer term economic progress. It must have been a benevolent weaver indeed who opted for a 75% reduction in income, a working pattern which all but eliminated their leisure and the accompanying lower life expectancy, greater prevalence of disease and all other aspects of Blake's Dark Satanic Mills, as a necessary cost for their unknown future generations' prosperity. We must not ask today's workers to make the same sacrifice.

ARE WE READY FOR THIS? WHAT COULD GO WRONG?

Firstly, let us answer this in a very simple way. We are not ready for this and a lot could go wrong! However, in order to prepare for the impact of the convergence of ABC on the world of work, we must further explore this simple question and answer.

In this book, we note the impacts on the world of work and the society in which we live of technological advancement, we note how the First Industrial Revolution wholly transformed the concept of work, and potentially more foundational ones such as time and money, progressing through history, we pinpointed a few key events and innovations, such as telegraph connectivity, beginnings of digitisation, the launch of the smart phone and so on. However, the changes that the worker now faces are unique in their pace. Earlier, with relation to cryptocurrency we noted how the evolution of money is now an online phenomenon with currency and whole financial infrastructures being developed, launched and incorporated in months and weeks, rather than decades, as previously happened. We would challenge workers to consider their own organisations and recount the technological changes, positive and negative, even over the last few years. It is highly likely if you work in a large organisation that over the last few years, you have seen whole functions hollowed out and replaced, reorganised or removed. It is highly likely that your human resources department, payroll and other back office functions have fewer staff and more online connectivity and services. You may well have noticed that organisational structures are becoming flatter around you, as middle managers may be being reutilised elsewhere. If you are at the point of sale, you will have undoubtedly noticed the huge lessening of cash you process and the way in which people pay will have changed. You may notice that sales cluster around the £30 point to allow for contactless payment, you may notice in retail that if you are in a store with a large online presence part of your role has been redesigned to process returns. You could see targets shifting towards collation of consumer data, and perhaps wonder why you have to give the option of an email receipt or attempt to collect the customers email address through competitions, after sales services or so on. You will have noticed the shift to online options of your products and potentially even a movement away from physical space. Retail units are shrinking, backs of stores more so. As stick holdings are reduced, it is expected that sales will be made online. Considering your retail space, you may note that experiential shopping is becoming much more commonplace and that your department store, now alongside clothing concessions, has coffee shops, fine dining and in at least one notable example a luxury car showroom, in the space where recently it sold children's clothes. Your customers are now part of the online ecosystem and are able to constantly feedback and comment. Even now, our world of work has changed considerably in the last half decade, and generally below this large-scale noticeable change there is a myriad of small scale, but just as impactful, change, impactful on the organisation, customer and the worker. The view and opinion of an organisation by its workers may now be extremely fluid; previous differences in view between different grades and roles exist, but are amplified by groups doing the same role, with the longer term staff permanent and the newer staff on temporary or fixed term contracts. Even for permanent staff, older contracts may have better clauses and conditions attached (where legal), older (better) pension schemes may be closed to new staff, older staff may have benefited from considerably more training and development, benefits and 'perks'.

We are still far from understanding the full effects of this change on society and the individual. We note with concern the increased spending patterns and propensity to debt associated with our psychological removal from our idea of money exacerbated by our technology. An individual receiving a real-time, personalised advertisement accompanied by offers of finance may find it increasingly hard to resist. Imagine a future where your perfect dream holiday, exactly tailored to your wants based on all your previous holiday searches, comments on your friends' holiday photographs and linked back to key events in your life, comes with a direct preapproved loan to fund it.

We generally talk of cultural lag, the notion that a society is generally behind the technology it adopts and that this causes often significant issues, with regard to a particular innovation. However, we can explore this idea with regard to the ABC economy we propose, and note that several foundational relationships between the worker and work may not survive. The idea of a career or job for life may be waning, but it is still often seen as aspirational. How will society function if the possibility of this is totally remote? The ideas of a single employer, a single skill set or of even knowing who you are working for may also fade. Work and society will change rapidly, quicker than ever before, and yet we are still relying on our very human society to keep up. To reiterate a key theme of this book, the state must provide the safety net, both financial and psychological, for the individual. Our human ability to cope with such change may be limited, and various behavioural biases and heuristics may make this more difficult. If we examine the sections above, a worker in an organisation, recognising the change, particularly of a flattened hierarchy may be consciously aware of this, but still convinced that they will be able to be promoted. If this social contract breaks down, and progression continues to be a removed option for many workers, then the consequences could be considerable and manifest in a variety of forms.

Society is not ready for the new way of working derived from the ABC economy, quite simply as concepts that will be removed (a speeding up of current trends) are quite rightly seen as valuable, and they are being replaced by ones which are traditionally considered undesirable.

So then, what could go wrong? The obvious lesson from the previous Industrial Revolution(s) is simple. Longer term the subsequent generation of workers may benefit, in the short term, the current workforce will generally lose pay, conditions, rights and satisfaction. Furthermore, workers displaced by new technologies or approaches will often never return back to the pay and conditions that they had previously. Crucially, a whole generation of workers may be 'in between', they may begin careers, train and invest in them and see their expected world of work disappear around them. This disappearance may well be subtle to start with. Their expected progression routes may disappear, wages may not keep up with inflation, training and upskilling options could no longer be available. Then, *en masse* we could see hiring freezes and redundancies, here we would see recession-type behaviours from employers and organisations, without the accompanying drops in economic activity. This economic paradox could continue, wholly displacing a generation of workers as the skills required by the new world of work are at best limited in this transitional generation. Even notions of transferrable skills provided through schooling, further and higher education are unlikely to suffice, as fundamentally the worker, or expectant worker, has devoted much of their skill set to a single, or at best a few, competencies. It is not just the skill deficit (or more accurately misalignment), but the approach, philosophy and behaviours of the transitional generation which will hamper their working in the new world of work. The stickiness in approach of our schooling and training institutions at an institutional and organisational level may well further exacerbate this as these institutions may, without state support and direction, continue to provide a traditional skill set. Indeed, it is all too easy to imagine a state education regulator hampering efforts of individual institutions to adapt and update their curricula to this end, the skills that may well be needed in this future of work are untried and untested, it is a courageous (or possibly reckless) body which embraces their teaching until the need is inarguably clear.

However, as we see it, the key danger of the new world of work we see as a potential outcome of the convergence of ABC, is that it can facilitate a complete global race to the bottom in terms of worker pay and conditions. Algorithms can reduce the skill required to complete an output or process by fundamental reduction of said output or process to a series of lower skilled tasks. Blockchain smart contracts and a reduction in physicality of work and geographic constraints can coordinate a system of underbidding for any particular task until the wage reaches the lowest subsistence price for labour. Furthermore, cryptocurrencies can both reduce options for the worker if a particular firm will only pay for a task in their own corporate cryptocurrency and potentially make state involvement in the monetary process harder. In this view of the ABC economy, then, wages and conditions have been competed down to subsistence levels only and the state is less able to provide worker protections or welfare due to their being edged out of the monetary process. A bleak future indeed, and closer to many of the dystopian pictures painted in science fiction books and films. Unfortunately, given our understanding of history, this is also far too believable.

It is again all too easy to imagine this on an international scale, just a few years ago, the potential for this bleak future was based around a relatively simple global analysis. Ultimately, a state or head of state would see a benefit from this degradation of pay and conditions. It may be for political ideology, a response to (or a threat to) the global order or simply as we have seen many times before, an attempt to lure global corporations or foreign investment. In any traditional analysis, this would spark a race to the bottom, not dissimilar to the rush to cut corporation taxes to attract business, where, once price (wage) competition is the norm, undercutting to win business, to a stage where no one can further undercut is the likely outcome. This however was in a stage of global order where national governments were acting in concert to approach (however unsatisfactorily) the pressing global challenges and emergencies. Here, we imagined the coordination of global powers, presenting a united front against the challenges of the ABC economy and the issues arrived around lone states refusing to participate and threating this approach. However, even through the writing of this book, that is becoming far harder to envisage. Deregulation and wage reduction, in this technological market place, in essence, at the whim of a political statement and accomplished at the increasing pace of the ABC economy, could easily 'bring jobs back', but at what cost for the worker?

RECOMMENDATIONS

Before we get to the overall recommendations, we must note the response of one anonymous reviewer who felt that we were advocating a future where holders of cryptocurrency would see increasing returns. That may be the case, or indeed the influx and future dominance of corporate cryptocurrencies may in effect remove potential returns to the lone investor, or as with any investment a myriad of unforeseen, unexpected and generally unknown events will affect the outcome. In terms of financial advice, we are giving none. Ultimately, should you decide to invest in cryptocurrency, the underlying blockchain technology or anything else, we only recommend that you seek appropriate financial advice.

Overall, then, and contrary to the overall philosophy of the initial cryptocurrencies of decentralisation and a removal of government from the economic process, we advocate a strong role for government, regulation and policy action. Much of the initial allure of cryptocurrencies was based around the removal of government from the monetary process, blockchain removes intermediaries and automation may remove worker protections. This wholesale removal of external bodies can in essence be twinned with the potential for wholesale removal of any worker rights, protections and surplus from the work process. Indeed, it is all too easy imagine a world where automation and algorithmising creates a world of work solely based on the necessary base process for each output, a de facto world of entirely unskilled work and where the lack of geographic constraints simply increases competition for each 'bit' of work to where (charitably) the price for that work falls simply to subsistence levels. In this world, smart contracts and instantaneous infinitely divisible payments combine to create a global work bank, who are in effect on zero-hour subsistence wage contracts. We could even go further, with the ability for algorithms to learn and adapt, the simple act of completing a piece of 'bit' work would generate more data on that process eventually leading to, via the 'data exploitation' of the Bitworker to a further reduction in the price for that piece of work due to efficiencies generated through the use of that additional data point. Unionisation would be next to impossible in its traditional form. Geographic freedoms and mass over supply of labour could create a race to the bottom and even international 'competition' based on diminishing worker protections and rights.

Ironically, part of the solution to this may lie in the development of corporate cryptocurrencies such as Libra. Notwithstanding the debates around the corporate incursion into what in effect is traditionally only the province of sovereign governments and nation states, the issuance of money and the generation of seigniorage, Libra and the Libra Council are known entities. In effect, they give this currency a face, an entity and governments a port of call. Libra has a defined working structure, a platform of operation and a series of whitepapers dictating its processes. For the first time, a mass cryptocurrency will have a structure regulatory bodies that can understand and incorporate into their functions. Libra has killed the initial crypto promise of decentralisation and all of its inherent dangers for governments, by in effect becoming just another currency. If we simply imagine the Libra Council as just another currency board, Libra in effect becomes mundane, and mundane becomes safe. Libra can be incorporated relatively easily into a nation states taxation regime and fiscal and monetary policies. The UK's National Insurance System should be able to, in effect handle an income or a portion of it in Libra as easily as it can handle a UK national who receives part of their income in Euros or Dollars. Corporate cryptocurrencies remove the decentralisation and thus danger of cryptocurrencies for the nation state and ironically may be vital for the prevention of the wholesale McDonaldisation of work. States must carefully choose between a powerful, but more limited in effect, challenge to their monetary dominance (corporate cryptocurrencies) and a weaker but potentially far more disruptive challenge (true decentralised cryptocurrencies). An unenviable decision, but one that will need to be made in the near future. Which way this goes could have significant implications for the world of work as well as the future of fiscal and monetary policy.

The following survival guide suggests individual level recommendations, however, it is worth spending a little time considering the wider economic affects and appropriate policy recommendations here.

The potential outcome of the ABC economy is, in our view, wholly transformative, the idea we discuss earlier, that a worker from today, were they transported into our proposed world of work, would find little familiarity, should give policy pause for thought. If this new world of work is as wholly different as we believe is possible, then the structures, organisations and safety nets of today are redundant. Throughout this book, we have noted that there is a bright potential future, which can only be realised if accompanied by farsighted, long-term and proactive policy. First and foremost, governments must acknowledge that the transition to this new way of working is more akin to rapid deindustrialisation rather than gradual technological change. Policy to protect the worker must be key, as must learning from failed policy in the past. In order to maintain prosperity and not increase (dare we dream to decrease) inequality, displaced workers must not lose out further. The displacement of the middle income worker must not be to lower wages and worse conditions. Graduates must not enter a transitioning labour market where their skills evaporate but their debt remains, and precarity must be addressed rather than become the norm. Mass training and technological upskilling must be a priority for any government, this training must be proactive and not a response to unemployment when the worker has already lost out, but training to allow a worker to evolve and adapt to their benefit within the new economy.

Additionally, clear and serious thought needs to be given to wider fiscal and monetary policy within this new world. In terms of personal taxation, one instinctively feels that the corporate cryptocurrencies (stablecoins) will pose less of a headache for governments than a myriad of transferrable and opaque tokens. However, this is only with regard to personal taxation, the transfer of monetary power from state to corporation may have a number of further issues for the global economy and may simply maintain the ability to tax the worker, but further increase the distance between the state's claims and the corporations willingness to pay. However, if indeed we journey to a world of heavily increased platform working, then considerations to the usual duties of the employer need to be made. In order to maintain conditions for the worker, the provision of pensions, insurance, holiday pay and so on must be maintained. In particular, we would recommend that pension contributions and crucially employer contributions are incorporated into any smart contract, with similar protections against opting out and incentives to save. It is a simple stretch of the imagination to consider that with smart contracts a worker can generate and maintain their own 'welfare and insurance' portfolio. However, the state must ensure that this is not simply a race to the bottom or a further widener of inequality by regulating a fair minimum where employers pay their share. Ultimately, the cost saving to the employer from their labour supply being platform based, must not simply (as history tells us is all too easy) be incorporated into short-term profitability, but be used to create long-term sustainable conditions for the Bitworker.

To summarise, key recommendations for government are as follows:

1. Long-term well considered regulation of cryptocurrencies.

2. Worker training and protections.

3. A blockchain welfare state.

4. State-supported (Digital) Trade Union(s).

Fundamentally, the future world of work is uncertain. Practical advice is therefore difficult to achieve in surety but must be attempted in order to deliver workable strategic advice today for the many stakeholders whom ABC will affect going forward.

Learners of today must consider the large-scale commoditisation of presently full and part-skilled professions when choosing their future careers. As previously discussed, it does not automatically follow that this will mean poorer pay and conditions. These detrimental impacts from the perspective of the worker tend only to be coupled with advancements in automations where tasks can largely be coded and thereby may replace human endeavour. However, where this is not the case, our ABCs can deliver more security over future income streams by forward selling Bitworker time. Students must therefore trade-off their career preferences against required future flexibility. However, what is clear is that there are little-to-no areas of work activity which this all-pervasive technology will not impact. Therefore, rather than seeking to run from such advancements, the best and continued advice would always be to study and aim to do what you are passionate about doing. Such passions are unlikely to feature the occupations outlined by Frey (2017) as being at risk from automation, for example, Data Entry Keyers, Library Technicians and New Accounts Clerks, etc. Instead, we would encourage students to aspire to more creative and higher order work activities such as artists, therapists, directors and consultants. A world with fewer rote accountants but more creativity (not creative accounting!), is likely to be one which delivers more worker satisfaction but whether this can deliver the required aggregate employment numbers to sustain an economy remains to be seen. In summary, work hard, follow what inspires you and ask yourself the your choice of profession could be automated to some extent. If 'yes', then be careful in your choice of vocation.

For those presently engaged in employment, we have previously highlighted key worker trends including: the fragmentation of worker tasks, the reduction of employed roles, the increasing rarity of a job for life and the threat of worker replacement due to automation. These trends are evident today and we see the effects of ABC as increasing them further still. If you are a worker in a role or industry at threat to automation then due consideration should be given to how this threat will be mitigated. Possible solutions include a career switch, upskilling in your present sector, or perhaps seeking to gain promotion to managerial or leadership roles which may prove to be more resilient to the aforementioned threats. Moreover, we would encourage workers to seek a portfolio of income streams where possible in order to better diversify their individual risk and allow them to take advantage of future flexibility both in terms of seising upside opportunities and defending against downside threats.

It would be glib to suggest that schools, colleges and universities should place an increased emphasis on skill development in areas such as coding and technology, etc. Indeed, this is already the case today and many initiatives have been launched to foster this desire. One such example is Scratch at www.scratch.mit.edu developed by Harvard Graduate School of Education which provides children with a basic programming language where they can build stories, music and animations whilst learning the basic structure and rules of a typical coding language. Given the nature of the technologies which we have envisioned it is key that teachers and lecturers build such learning in to all layers of most educational courses similar to that of ethics or sustainability which are often incorporated across all units of study given their pervasive importance. The corollary of the above would be a focus upon increasingly creative subjects including, but not limited to, creative writing, leadership, music and the arts more broadly. However, such subjects have typically been squeezed of late attracting increasingly smaller allocations of already dwindling pots of funding. Economic pressures often necessitate such changes especially given a world which places greater importance, status and employment prospects upon Science Technology Engineering and Mathematics (STEM) subjects. A balance here is obviously key as there is little advantage in training a generation of poets with little regard for how these individuals can find meaningful employment post their educational pathways.

Small business owners above all stakeholder groups stand to gain perhaps most from the technological advancements which we have critically discussed above. Smart contracts will deliver greater confidence in cash flow management ensuring payment is obtained in good time and thereby helping business to plan with confidence and grow accordingly.

Furthermore, the increasing commoditisation and availability of flexible working will allow Small to Medium sized Enterprises (SMEs) to more easily flex their employment resources in line with their business needs. This helps to keep operational gearing at relatively lower levels which in turn reduces risk for the owner manager. In contrast to the above advantages, the ABCs of our triumvirate are likely to disrupt and shorten many supply chains which may negate the need, and even perhaps the existence, of many smaller organisations.

FINAL THOUGHTS

In *Algorithms, Blockchain & Cryptocurrency: Implications for the Future of the Workplace*, we have made a series of (hopefully) logical assumptions and suppositions based upon ongoing and emerging trends and supertrends both in the study of work and in the wider global economy. We must however acknowledge the considerable issues of future forecasting. During the writing of this book, the once inevitable march of the corporate cryptocurrency appears to be being (at least temporarily) derailed. As discussed in greater detail in the recommendations section, the 'likely' issuance of a global cryptocurrency is a key feature of our proposed ABC economy and analysis of its implications for the future of work. We ultimately believe that the 'Genie is out of the bottle' for these types of currencies and their eventual issuance will affect the future of working. Clearly, though, the timings are far less clear and dependable than they were in early 2019. In practice, then, for the book and the future as written, we may well see the themes presented coming to pass in a very similar timescale. There is a strong possibility that Big Tech, a GAFA or a BAT or even an emerging entity, will learn the lessons of Libra and utilising a 'send mover advantage' successfully launch a global corporate cryptocurrency in Libra's image and maybe with a smoother regulatory ride. It appears that elements of the trust in Big Tech which has generally outweighed the trust in traditional banking firms post 2008 crisis, is waning. It is this trust which also provides a foundation for the movement towards what we have termed the ABC economy. The current (October 2019 at the time of writing) increasing scrutiny of social media as we move towards democratic events in the UK and USA is shaking the trust in these technologies and firms, especially in the demographics which are 'the workers of tomorrow'. Barely a day goes by without further revelations around the intrusion, privacy and wellbeing issues arising from social media, continual web connection and the over-arching issue of technological progression outpacing cultural and societal ability to adapt. The stage here is being set for increasing societal, and regulatory pressures on the role and infiltration of tech in the world of work, and the future revelations revealed by this scrutiny may well further shake the trust in ABC, prompting unforeseen adaptions and adoptions of technology outside the scope of this book. The notions of trust in society are highly relevant here, the reported issues surrounding Cambridge Analytica and their dissemination to the wider public, the frequent notifications of missing cryptocurrency and its continued association with crime further serve to reduce societal trust in these technologies. However, the future we outline relies on trust in order to operate, we note that blockchain 'replaces trust with truth', and if societal trust wanes in Big Tech to such an extent, that the transparent, immutable and verifiable properties of blockchain and associated smart contracts become the only mechanism facilitating the economy, then we question, if giving existing trust dynamics, this will be enough to promote wholesale change in the world of work.

Yet, technological change in the world of work continues apace, we can see numerous examples of the burgeoning use of smart contracts, a worrying continuation of flexibility without stability in work (precarity), a rise in self-employment and platform working. We can see the foundations for a positive amalgamation of tech and work, however the positive outcome which is beneficial for all, is perhaps becoming more elusive.

To conclude, in agreement with the themes expressed in this book, Christine Lagarde, President of The European Central Bank recently (December 2019) explained that:

> *My personal conviction is that given the developments that we are seeing, not so much in the Bitcoin segment, but in the stablecoins projects – and we only know of one at the moment but there are others being explored and underway at the moment – we'd better be ahead of the curve, if that happens, because there is clearly a demand out there that we have to respond to.*

REFERENCES

Bagus, P. (2003), Deflation: When Austrians become interventionists, *The Quarterly Journal of Austrian Economics*, 6(4), 19–35.

Choi, Y., & Phan, P. (2006). A generalized supply/demand approach to national entrepreneurship: examples from the United States and South Korea. In D. Demougin & C. Schade (Eds.), *Entrepreneurship, marketing, innovation: an economic perspective on entrepreneurial decision making* (pp. 11–34). Berlin: Duncker & Humblot Verlag.

Davidson, S., De Filippi, P., & Potts, J. (2018). Blockchains and the economic institutions of capitalism. *Journal of Institutional Economics*, 14(4), 639–658.

Financial Services Authority (FSA). (2009). *The Turner review: A regulatory response to the global banking crisis*, London.

Frey, C. B. (2019). *The technology trap: Capital, labor, and power in the age of automation*. Princeton, NJ: Princeton University Press.

Frey, C. B., & Osborne, M. A. (2017). The future of employment: How susceptible are jobs to computerisation? *Technological Forecasting and Social Change*, 114(January), 254–280.

Gertchev, N. (2004). Dehomogenizing Mises' monetary thought. *Journal of Libertarian Studies*, 18(3).

Haddad, C., Haddad, C., Hornuf, L. & Hornuf, L. (2019). The emergence of the global fintech market: economic and technological determinants. *Small Business Economics, 53*(1), 81–105.

Halpern, S. (2018). Bitcoin Mania. *The New York Review of Books, 65*(1), 52, 54, 56.

Hayek, F. A. (1937). Investment that raises demand for capital. *Review of Economics and Statistics, 19*(4).

Hayek, F. A. (1969). Three elucidations of the Ricardo effect. *The Journal of Political Economy, 77*(2), 274–285.

Hayek, F. A. (1975). The paradox of saving. In *Profits, interest and Investment and other essays on the theory of industrial fluctuations*. Clifton, NJ: August M Kelly Publishers.

Hayek, F. A. (2007). *Denationalisation of money*. Institute of Economic Affairs (reprint of 1976 issue).

Herbener, J. M. 2002, After the Age of inflation: Austrian proposals for monetary reform, *The Quarterly Journal of Austrian Economics, 5*(4), 5–19.

Hodgson, G. (2015). *Conceptualizing Capitalism*. Chicago, IL: University of Chicago Press.

Hülsmann, J. G. (2008), Mises on Monetary Reform: the Private Alternative, *The Quarterly Journal of Austrian Economics, 11*(3), 208–218.

Iansiti, M., & Lakhani, K.R. (2017). The truth about blockchain. *Harvard Business Review, 95*(1), 118–127.

Miller, R. (2009). The Austrians and the Crisis. *Institute of Economic Affairs Journal Compilation*. Oxford: Blackwell Publishing.

Mises, L. (1966). *Human action, a treatise on economics*. Henry Regnery Company by arrangement with Yale University Press, Indianapolis.

Mises, L. (1980). *Theory of money and credit*. Indianapolis, IN: Liberty Classics.

Muller, A. P. (2001). Financial cycles, business activity and the stock market. *Quarterly Journal of Austrian Economics, 4*(1), 3–21.

Nakamoto, S. (2008). Bitcoin: A peer-to-peer electronic cash system. Cryptography Mailing list at https://metzdowd.com.

Pessoa, J. P., & Van Reenen, J. (2014). The UK productivity and jobs puzzle: does the answer lie in wage flexibility?. *The Economic Journal, 124*(576), 433–452.

Rothbard, M. N. (2001). *The case for a 100 percent gold dollar*. Cambridge, MA: Harvard University Press (1962, reprint by the Ludwig Von Mises Institute).

Salerno, J. T. (2010). *Money: Sound and unsound*. Auburn, AL: Ludwig von Mises Institute.

Selgin, G. A. (1988). *The theory of free banking: Money supply under competitive note issue*. Totowa, NJ: Rowman and Littlefield.

Sennholz, H. F. (1985). *Money and freedom*. Spring Mills, WV: Libertarian Press.

Sennholz, H. F. (1987). *Debts and deficits*. Spring Mills, WV: Libertarian Press

de Soto, J. (2006). In M. A. Stroup (Trans.), *Money, bank credit and economic cycles*. Auburn, AL: Ludwig von Mises Institute.

de Soto, J. (2009). *Money, bank credit and economic cycles*. Auburn, AL: Ludwig von Mises Institute.

de Soto, J. (2010). Economic recessions, banking reform and the future of capitalism. LSE Hayek Memorial Lecture Transcript provided by the Mises Institute (originally published by the Cobden Centre).

Spithoven, A. (2019), Theory and Reality of Cryptocurrency Governance, *Journal of Economic Issues*, 53(2), 385–393.

Tokenomy. (2019). Central bank digital currencies (CBDCs): Where do we go from here? Published by The Medium App on 4th September 2019. https://medium.com/@tokenomy/central-bank-digital-currencies-cbdcs-where-do-we-go-from-here-546186486ebd. Accessed on 28 October 2019.

Van den Hauwe, L. (2006). *Review of Huerta de Soto's Money, Bank Credit and Economic Cycles. Munich Personal RePEc Archive*. MPRA Paper no. 49, Posted November 7, 2007.

White, L. (1989). *Competition and currency*. New York, NY: New York University Press.

White, W. R. (2008), Past financial crises, the current financial turmoil, and the need for a new macrofinancial stability framework, *Journal of Financial Stability*, 4(4), 307–312.

Zimmermann, G. (2003). Austrian monetary policy views: A short critique, *The Quarterly Journal of Austrian Economics*, 6(4), 77–80.

INDEX

Note: Page numbers followed by "*n*" indicate notes.